COMPLETING THE PICTURE

– *Stride* –

Other Stride anthologies:

A Curious Architecture: a selection of contemporary prose poems
edited by David Miller and Rupert Loydell

How The Net Is Gripped: a selection of contemporary American Poetry
edited by David Miller and Rupert Loydell

The Stumbling Dance: 21 poets
edited by Rupert M. Loydell

The Rainbow's Quivering Tongue: an anthology of women's poetry
edited by Mary Plain

Jewels & Binoculars: fifty poets celebrate Bob Dylan
edited by Phil Bowen

Stonechat: ten Devon poets
edited by Christopher Southgate

Ladder To The Next Floor: Stride Magazine 1-33
edited by Rupert M. Loydell
(University of Salzburg Press)

Other Stride books by authors in this anthology:

Northwoods Peter Dent

A Banquet For Rousseau David H.W. Grubb

The Rain Children David H.W. Grubb

Coal John Gurney

Safe Levels Alexis Lykiard

Leaving The Corner: Selected Poems 1973-1985 Brian Louis Pearce

Jack o'Lent Brian Louis Pearce

Other Stride books by the editor:

Mad Tom On Tower Hill

Cardboard Troy

COMPLETING THE PICTURE

exiles, outsiders & independents

edited by
William Oxley

COMPLETING THE PICTURE

First edition 1995

ISBN 1 873012 91 8

Cover design by Joe Pieczenko.

Published by
Stride Publications
11 Sylvan Road, Exeter,
Devon EX4 6EW

Contents

'Do I contradict myself?
Very well then I contradict myself,
(I am large, I contain multitudes.)'
– Whitman: *Song Of Myself.*

'The lyf so short, the craft so long to lerne,'
– Chaucer: *Parlement of Foules.*

Introduction

Over the years of my involvement with the British poetry world I have become aware of a number of poets who, for one reason or another, have seemed always to be somehow 'on the wrong foot'. Some of these poets are well-known; others less-so: though it is clearly not to the point, for fame – or its absence – seems to have little to do with the lack of critical reception accorded them. (Fame may, of course, get poets jobs in creative writing, or as judges of poetry competitions, or readings etc., but this by itself does not ensure they become the subject of serious critical attention.) It is not a matter of these poets being part of a labelable movement such as 'the avant-garde', or 'post-modernism' – which may be disagreeable to whatever establishment it is that determines poetic reputations. For all the poets I have gathered together in this anthology have nothing in common save their individuality and capacity to turn out excellent work on occasion. If that work, in turn, has anything in common beyond its quality it is as a recognizable continuation of the tradition of English poetry. Which is to say: their work is more tinged with a traditionalist approach than with the very real anti-traditionalism which characterises, in its extreme form, the truly avant-garde. And although their work has, for example in Pearce and Russell, absorbed the more valuable lessons of modernism, none of the poets would subscribe to such dictum as 'language is the only reality', or practise the thorough-going impressionist technique (although some have flirted with it) of what is currently termed 'post-modernism'. Though Pound argued that 'technique is a test of sincerity', I do not believe that any of these poets, however experimental some may have been at times, have ever suffered from what Robert Graves called 'technosis' – that sickness affecting every department of modern society, including language itself.

So why have these relatively traditionalist poets been for so long (in some cases very long) wrong-footed in critical esteem? I think there are a number of reasons.

In the first place, criticism is itself to blame. For these poets – paradoxically like many poets who have more easily earned acceptance – have fallen victim to our century's principal critical error: that of confounding author and work. This is something which can often work, in the short term, to the poet's advantage: although almost always in the long term to his or her disadvantage – hence my use of the word 'paradox'. Sound criticism judges the poem not the poet; or, in Lawrence's phrase, 'trusts the song not the singer'. Today, and for some years now, all kinds of extraneous factors like 'youth', 'race', 'politics', 'personal notoriety', 'gender', 'sexual orientation', etc., have been permitted to distort critical judgement, with the result that talent has been arbitrarily elevated or depressed with an astonishing regularity in the domain of poetry. Of course, 'the better' will always be at war with 'the best' in any age; and critical detachment will not always be maintained, for various reasons; but never has it been so difficult as in our century for genuine talent, let alone genius, to get a 'fair crack of the whip'. This despite Matthew Arnold's solemn warning to foster detachment of judgement as much as possible.

That said, however, the parlous state of contemporary criticism is not more to blame for the situation this anthology seeks to redress than the poets themselves. Responsibility has to be shared: self-imposed exile (or its stay-at-home equivalent of being an outsider), for however good a reason, is the other major factor in the equation leading to critical non-acceptance. In an age dominated by what Robert Graves called 'the career poet' (perhaps more accurately today 'the designer poet' – that cynosure of the creative writing workshop), exiled and outsider poets may feel doubly justified for having chosen the path of the recluse. Nevertheless, the decision is theirs.

Dannie Abse once observed 'poets are naturally subversive'. But their subversiveness is not simply that of surrender to the 'imp of perversity' which Edgar Allan Poe once referred to in one of his stories. It is, in fact, a habit of mind, this subversiveness, a way of thinking designed not primarily to subvert any social status quo, but to protect the poet's own position as artist. Poets (and other artists) are instinctive subversives, exiles, outsiders as a by-product of their propensity for original thinking.

It is sufficient to point to the fact of avoidance of cliché in expression, a tendency to question all received opinion, and a predilection towards imaginative envisioning over reality, as proof enough of an *ur* state of mind that leads poets and other artists to become exiles within or without society. As I once put it in a long poem (called, appropriately for this thesis, 'The Exile') the poet is 'an élitist who abhors all cliques of more than one'. I mean by 'the poet', of course, the genuine individual poet who wishes to think for him or herself: the poet whose work MacDiarmid was thinking of when he wrote 'Great work cannot be combined with surrender to the crowd' – sentiments echoed everywhere in the great Elizabethans, especially Shakespeare. This is not intellectual snobbery, or anything as cheap as literary politics, it is simply that the genuine poet or artist must clear a space in which to work and think, and attempt to be original as much as is humanly possible. The same too, of course, applies to the mystic who needs retreat to find God, or the scientist who needs a laboratory for experiment and research.

Because the poet's subject is the whole of life itself, there is unfortunately no simple retreat designable for the poet as a satisfactory social mechanism – no laboratory or church or monastery (or poetry society!) with the result that the poet's life becomes his or her retreat: their 'exile'. No one can share a poet's study but his muse and his god... or goddess; or, for the female poet, her daimon.

It is not possible for me to presume to speak for any of the poets in this selection. The one claim I would make for them and their poetry is that it reflects a far wider conspectus of universal concern with ideas and experience than many of the more publicised poets of today whose main concern seems to be *to conform to a style of streetwise verse writing* to the neglect of wider and deeper sensitivities. There are no role models here for the poetic lager lout! What I seek to do in this introduction is to suggest, by brief analysis, that their critical status – or, rather, their marginalisation – has been in large measure due to their integrity as exiles. Whether exiles 'way out in the centre', to borrow another phrase of Abse's, as in the case of Kathleen Raine firmly at home in Chelsea, but still very much the spiritual exile; or Francis Warner who has spent his creative life in the Groves of Academia in Oxford and Cambridge; or Peter Russell who has been firmly self-exiled 'anywhere but England' since the Sixties; or Brian Louis Pearce who has soldiered bravely on in the obscurity of darkest Twickenham, I am firmly convinced that some variant of exile status has kept all the contributors to this volume a long way off from critical recognition, if not always wholly out of the public eye.

One would like to think that after at least four centuries of approaching something like democracy, England, the land of 'fair-play', would have in its intellectual life (if nowhere else) developed a justly discriminating critical system and ethos. A climate which would, equally automatically, reject any and all factors extraneous to, and inimical of, the making of sound critical evaluation. But this has not happened. At best, the genuine art work only makes its appearance in the most haphazard and fitful way.

In preparing this anthology I have become aware of all sorts of ideas and factors contributing to this state of affairs. Not the least of which being, as I have suggested, that the responsibility for 'exile' lies always in some measure with the exiled. In each of the brief prefaces on the poets included I have sought to suggest or highlight some reason for the particular poet's neglect. Poetic neglect, of course, has many causes. One of the most frequent is due to what I would term 'the ignorance of the age', through which different generations tend to stick together critically: so that, for a poet, it becomes simply a matter of if he or she hasn't 'made it' in their generation then they've 'had it' for the present. Either one is an Auden/Heaney or a Blake/Hopkins. Yet the fact remains that many poets go on producing their best work over several generations, as posterity often recognizes.

The criticism that does exist today has become increasingly affected by media practices. In effect, the history of criticism – at least in the last fifty years – has become confused with the history of publicity. This is the only way to really account for the bright but brief 'stardom' of, for example, Brian Patten and Jeni Couzyn in the 1960s, Andrew Motion and Craig Raine in the 1970s/80s; and, very likely, the recently hyped Wendy Cope and Simon Armitage. While such poets are in the limelight, few people seem to be able to perceive in their work those factors (such as a too-slick contemporaneity) which makes them eminently forgettable in the longer term. Of course, one doesn't seek willingly to be at all unkind in such observations, but the truth is never kind to everyone... anymore than it will be to all in this anthology.

Because of critical neglect there is a tendency for such 'exiled' poets to over-produce. John Gurney is a good case in point here: such neglect has inspired him to the production of a monumental corpus of work: almost as many verse plays as Shakespeare (most, if not all, of them unperformed to date), plus thousands of sonnets and several gigantic epics. Again, critical neglect accounts, in no small measure I believe, for the dogmatic Platonism at work in the embattled, quasi-religious world created by Kathleen Raine. The sheer, even grandiose, anti-establishmentarianism of Peter Russell, combined with a whole library-swallowing Poundlike pursuit of erudition, is due to the unwillingness of what critical establishment exists (in and out of the academy) to give his work a fair hearing. More odd, but not dissimilar, is the case of Tom Scott, arguably the most considerable Scottish poet after Hugh MacDiarmid in that land of Lallans, Scots' nationalism, and radical politics: a poet eminently assimilable politically and culturally, he has never been anything but an outsider in his own land.

A further consequence of this tendency for such poets to over-produce is to become more and more widely published in little magazines and fugitive periodicals. (And though little magazines are the most valuable nurturing place for poetic talent, they are also the dumping ground for failed abilities and second-rate work – even of first-rate writers!) This can become counter-productive, because more and more work which should have appeared nowhere but in the wastepaper basket, will become public, and even genuine critics will feel, seeing such stuff, justified in neglecting further the already neglected. But this is a somewhat complex point, not only because many established poets (the late Roy Fuller is a good example) continue to loyally support little magazines, but because, in the words of Rupert Loydell, some poets are, quite simply, 'resolutely small press'; and some, at least, of my stratum of genuine but neglected poets may appear, at first sight, to fall into the latter category. To this near-conundrum there can be no real solution other than that provided by the good poem wherever it manages to see the light of day. Indeed, the one salutary thought ever to keep in mind when trying to anthologise is the example of F.T. Palgrave – perhaps the most successful anthologist ever – who never hesitated to mix the one-good-poem poet like Henry Carey with the likes of William Shakespeare.

Many poets, readers, and critics, have been struck for some time now just how *unrepresentative*, not only of that nebulosity 'the zeitgeist' but of genuine quality English poetry, such anthologies as Robert Conquest's *New Lines*, Alvarez's *New Poetry*, or the Motion-Morrison anthology of *Contemporary British Poetry* have been. But they are there, and false landmarks though they may be (and are in my view), the purpose of this anthology is neither to combat nor compete with them, but rather to widen the franchise and so help complete the picture. This is not an anti-establishment anthology so much as a non-establishment anthology.

No anthology, even one in some measure 'thematic', can hope to include everyone whom it might be thought had a claim for inclusion. In any case, an anthologist is, of necessity, limited in the comprehensiveness of his or her knowledge of possible candidates for such an anthology – and none more so than this anthologist. However, readers may be interested to know some of the poets whom I did consider but finally rejected, and my reasons for doing so. A very obvious candidate was Thom Gunn, but I decided not to approach him for work for he is far from being a 'neglected' poet. I thought about James Brockway, very much the geographical exile, having lived for many years in Holland, but known better for his translation work. Also, my terms of reference from the publisher required that my contributors had something of a track record of published volumes of their own poetry (a rule I have abided by in all cases) and, as far as I am aware, Brockway has not published any such volumes; or if he has, not for a very long time. In addition, I considered several well-known poets of small press reputations, but in the end decided that they were poets who had over-published in small magazines (see my comments above). Lastly, I gave considerable thought to John Powell Ward, who has been toiling at the margins of recognition for many years. But though Ward is, much as Auden was, a poet of immense verbal skills, I decided I could not quite make a case for him because, though he is an Englishman most associated with the Anglo-Welsh poetry scene and, thereby, a sort of 'exile', such did not seem quite a sufficient reason to argue for his inclusion. As to what may be said to constitute a 'sufficient reason' consistent with any thesis, well, such is a matter of informed opinion. But I decided not to approach the poet and Oxford don A.L. Rowse who, like Francis Warner, has with similar determination led a cloistered life, because I felt that one such 'exiled' representative of the academic world was sufficient – especially as the space at my disposal was not unlimited. Similarly, I considered the much younger academic Peter Abbs, not so much as an exile but as an independent spirit who has gone his own way for many years; a fine poet who, at last, has managed – with his volume *Icons Of Time* – to receive some critical attention: a remarkable feat for a mostly self-published author. There are a number of poets who, technically-speaking, fall within my terms of reference, but who, though poets, are better known in some other genre. For example, with the occasional exception, I find that where a poet has given a great deal of his or her time to, say, translating, their own poetry often suffers in some noticeable way.

Some may think it eccentric, but I wish to represent my 'exiles' and 'outsiders' – be they social, geographical, or merely 'inner exiles' – by a few good poems each. Recognising that to do anything like justice to a full conspectus of each poet's work is quite beyond the scope of this anthology, I have settled for presenting what I consider good poems as my criteria of evidence. This, rather than either a lengthy dissertation about my criteria for deciding what is a good poem; or detailed claims about the critical status of the poets themselves: other than those which emerge in the brief biographies preceding each section. In other words, I prefer to allow the poems chosen to speak for themselves and for their authors, rather than make all sorts of general claims for the poets. If, by the method I have adopted, I do anything to lessen their critical marginalisation, then I shall be satisfied that the effort was worthwhile.

William Oxley

Anna Adams

b. 1926 in Surrey; an artist and ceramicist as well as a poet; she is married to Norman Adams, R.A. Her residences have oscillated between North Yorkshire sheep country; Burlington House, London; and Newcastle. Like Kathleen Raine, a London childhood was followed by a lot of the North. A dedicated craftswoman, Anna Adams has – like all in this volume – soldiered long on the margins of critical attention. Despite her work finding reputable publishers such as Peterloo and Littlewood; despite strong contacts with the Arts Establishment, she remains an isolated figure 'way out in the centre'. It is in her craft, that lapidary, Heaney-like use of words, the solid music of her metres, combined with a distinctly exploratory, often ruminative voice, that Adams' strength has always been. Her weakness lies less in craft than subject: too many of her poems seem merely skilful descriptions (e.g. much of her volume *Trees In Sheep Country*). A good poet needs some obsession other than just writing poems or painting pictures – a sort of message or vision – like Pound with his Douglasite economics, or Kathleen Raine with her *religio perennis*. For all her skills, Anna Adams seems not to have this. Perhaps an anti-romantic, anti-mythological (those 'visioned woods / that spring from magic themes') bias has pushed her into a sort of secular, unspiritual *impasse*? Perhaps this is why she has turned so often to the paintings of others for vision and to nature for nourishment? Whatever the reasons, it is time her work was subjected to a proper critical grilling, rather than being permitted to languish by default. Although any poet finds such an examination painful, it is usually beneficial in the long run for their work.

BLACK-HOUSE WOMAN.

1.

I am, myself, the house that shelters them.
My nerves extend into this skirt of stone,
this shawl of thatch. These windows are my eyes.
I am a hollow room, enfolding men.

The peat fire is my heart. This hearth is warm
always, for them, but through the open door
sometimes shy happiness steals in to me.
The sun lays yellow carpets on the floor.

My children bring home hunger, men bring storm,
and I absorb in quiet the sea-bird's cry,
the breaker's roar, till in the sleeping room
oceans and mountains lie.

They leave no room for me in my own womb;
by them, and by their dreams, my lap is filled;
I spread my skirts to shield them, I am home,
content to be my one forgotten child.

2.

They were my life; what is the use of me
now that my fire is out? I smell of soot
not smoke, wear dock and ragwort in my hat,
importune passing mountains of proud sea.

A broken thistle mutters by the bay
that winds have stolen all the seed she bore.
Mine also. Though roof-ribs, laid bare, declare
me dead, wormriddled, far gone in decay,

my emptiness craves fulness, as the shore
craves the returning tide. I welcome birds,
cherish the weaving spider, suckle weeds;
lacking my lord let nettles crowd my door.

A BURIAL AT HORTON

The last of our adopted fathers, now –
on this green-island day, amid wild snows –
after an absence has come back for good
to lay his big, slow-moving farmer's bones
in Horton churchyard where schoolfellows lie
under the disappearing local names:
    Bill Redmayne, Mason Baines, Beck Heseltine.

You started up at Dub Cote, with one horse,
then marvelled that you owned the Squire's old house
and worked a double farm. Hard work did well,
but you're set in the past now, with the Squire,
and lines of men with rakes to turn green swathes
to hay, and Mary Ellen bringing tea,
    and all the fragrant grass of eighty years.

When we first came, your son was newly wed;
then, hand in hand, over the emerald ground,
he and his bride walked out to tend the lambs.
Now my first son, then crying like a lamb,
is grown through more than twenty lambing-times
and gone away, leaving his ghost behind
    with this year's children fishing in the beck.

The snowdrifts underline the drystone walls.
Olympian plaster mountains stare, aloof,
over green drumlin hills where you're at home:
where "more snow comes to fetch old drifts away"
and "it's two topcoats colder on the fells"
and "never right warm when yon mountain's white",
    and you were born, and knew thy way about.

You gave their first pay-packets to my boys
one haytime, and you said they worked like men.
Were they about sixteen? They came home late
on Summer nights bright with the haytime moon,
blind-drunk on work, and milk dipped from the churn,
and supper on the newly-shaven ground,
    smelling of sweat and hayseeds, oil, machines.

Those lads are in the past now, with the men
of the old village, who were lads with you
in this green hammock slung from those white peaks,
and children playing games along "the Flat"
before the lorries commandeered all roads
such as the winding, one-way, switchback track
    that brought us here and will not take us back.

Your Sabbath-keeping used to rest the horse,
but tractors broke the custom. Breaking down,
machines kept random sabbaths of their own.
You mastered barns full of the new machines
but change from hay to silage finished you,
moving your landmarks round while you stood by.
    A full-time Sabbath claimed you in the end.

Stealing your cautious smile and careful thought
out of our sight and into history,
the plodding pace of one who walks all day
and never hurries, brought you to this place
where you are folded in, under the turf
spread with snow-fleeces, like a shearing ground,
    beside your wife, among the village names.

Bill Redmayne: Mason Baines: Beck Heseltine:
Jack Lambert, John, Meg in her haytime hat:
John Dinsdale, Dinsdale daughters, let Bob in.
The village of his boyhood swings its gate.
The grave heals first with snow, and then with grass:
then with forgetfulness. New villagers
    we shuffle up towards the empty place.

DRAGONFLY CONSIDERS HELICOPTER

for Chris O'Toole

Some say the idol Screw-Wing is our god
    but I am not fooled
and will not be fobbed off with mined and made

toys of newfangled Man. We are too old.

Machines are forgeries that cannot think;
with dreaming minds
we cling, right-angled, to the sedge, our link
with half-forgotten ponds

where many times our wingless souls have lived.
My fishbowl head
is like a divers' helmet. I have dived
repeatedly, and been new-made from mud.

Sedge is our birth-cord from the watery bag
into the summer skies;
resting from flight that flashed zigzag, zigzag,
I praise our beauty, and my compound eyes

compare the noisy Screw-Wing overhead
with us, the seminal thought
from slow Creation's carboniferous bed.
A pseudo-insect's lifespan must be short.

We posture on the sedges like straight flags –
we Devil's Darners –
clasping our rungless ladders with six legs
of brittle chitin bent at flexy corners

so that our jewelled tails lie horizontal.
Glass wings unfurled,
I hold my pose with pride in fundamental
knowledge. I'm the linch-pin of the world.

Sebastian Barker

b. 1945; degrees from the universities of Oxford and East Anglia; son of the poet George Barker and the poet-novelist Elizabeth Smart. Employments: carpenter, fireman, Sotheby's cataloguer, arts administrator, etc. One of the few poet-philosophers around: a generous, complex, charismatic man, Barker has perhaps been 'wrong-footed' like, for another example Omar Pound, and for the same reason: only gradually struggling out from under parental shades of achievement to claim, latterly, his share of the limelight through the publication of his well-received epic verse-biography of Nietszche. Until recently, Sebastian Barker was also chairman of the Poetry Society, steering it through one of the most difficult periods in its history; he has also been on the executive committee of P.E.N. Something of a committee man, then? Well, not long ago I met a photographer in the provinces who averred knowledge of the poet in his 'wilder youth', and expressed surprise that Barker should have 'become a pillar of the Establishment'. For me this only testifies to his complexity of character which, on the technical level, manifests itself not so much in the irregularity of his line within poems (he is a formalist), but in the irregularity of line between poems. Rather like Blake, Sebastian Barker tends to oscillate between the simple lyric of the *Songs Of Innocence* and the prolixity of the Prophetic Books. Never averse to the long poem, a certain indecisiveness of line (c.f. the volume *Poems*, 1974) has meant that he has had some difficulty in developing and maintaining a rhythm: a problem which – for all the revision which went into it – his Nietszche book, *The Dream Of Intelligence* (1992), has not entirely solved. But as a poet of cosmic range of concern in an age of trivial themes, Sebastian Barker is certainly outstanding and almost unique. For this reason alone he deserves the sympathetic aid of the critical toothcomb rather than its total non-use.

TILTY MILL

Can I ever return again
To where I can never go,
To the dark green woods by the fields
Where the tall grasses grow?

Can I ever return again
To the child I was before
When I lay by the rippling water
And the dappled light on the shore?

For ever and ever amen
I am delighting there
While the sun on the wooden wheel
And the millstream arc through the air..

HUNGOVER IN HENLEY

Antique England sizzles in
Coloured snapshots on the high.
Silver tongs and rolling pin
Feed the proud nostalgic eye.

Copper kettle, feathered hat,
Printed linen, jelly mould,
One-eighty-thou a freehold that
Red dot indicates is sold.

Floury loaves, meringues, old wine,
Cotton aprons, coffee shoppes,
Patchwork cushions, polished pine,
And a glass jar of snowdrops.

Buttered muffins, flintwork church,
Elizabethan timber-frames,
Higgledy graves, a dancing birch,
And I'm in alcoholic flames.

BLUEBELLS

I know I make a symbol
Of the foxglove on the wall.
It is because it knows you.
– W.S. Graham

She had a place to go and went
Like spirit stepping from its case.
I saw her battered body spent
And nothing living in its place.
Unshaken by this cruel twist
She has a place to go and sing,
For she is forever there with us
Where bluebells come up in the spring.

In shaded dells where no one goes,
And valleys where the heron flies;
By hedges where the pale dogrose
And blackbirds countenance the skies;
In every speck of sun or dust
She has a place to be and sing,
For she is forever there with us
Where bluebells come up in the spring.

The river winding through the hills
Redeeming paradise on Earth;
The ecstasy of love which kills
The unborn child before its birth;
The atom's astronomic hiss:
Gave her two extremes to sing,
For she is forever there with us
Where bluebells come up in the spring.

A jaded parson walks the street,
The brazier by the tramp's defunct,
The blasted rows of houses reek
Of faeces where the rats have slunked;
Toddlers learn to take the piss,
And policemen on the gibbets swing,
Though she is forever there with us
Where bluebells come up in the spring.

The rich imprisoned by their wealth
(The poor imprisoned by it thrive)
Approach world politics with stealth
And murder while they're still alive.
It's hell on Earth. Injustice is.
And yet the poor may hear her sing,
For she is forever there with us
Where bluebells come up in the spring.

The creeping sly delinquent fool
Fashions music out of verse
And thinks he'll teach the ruling school
How much his harmonies are worth.
Untutored in the art of fuss
He hasn't taught his pain to sing,
Though she is forever there with us
Where bluebells come up in the spring.

The cloistered judge, bewigged and wise,
Drinking serenely on his own,
Has had enough of people's lies
And warms a heart as cold as stone.
The echoes fade of conscience, lust.
Off guard he hears a poet sing,
For she is forever there with us
Where bluebells come up in the spring.

The saint alone in blood and gore
Among the matrix of the time
Red-handed takes the pulse of war
And bandages the chests of pain.
The victims, living, take their place
Back where the bullets louder sing,
And she is forever there with us
When bluebells come up in the spring.

ST. AGNE. IN DEFIANCE OF AN ABSTRACTION

I feel comfortable in this village,
A man-atom in a soul-cleansing,
Drawing diagrams, doodling, marking time.
    What was the purpose of my life
Before I was born? Did the infinite
Spiral my being, like a mad
Astronaut, going nowhere, or did I
Have a purpose, before that gate-crashing?
    Here, in a green rain, where the trees
Drip their silver letters to the earth,
I engage with that Bastard-at-Arms,
Who, without flinch, torments me to this hour.
    Peace is the conquest of the evil power
Both in the mind and in the fruity earth;
It is the richness of the buried vaults
Both in the mind and in the fruity earth.
    But time, without cessation, haunts me here,
Bending my purpose to its bitter will;
Yet I, conqueror of the man-atom I am,
Defy this foot-soldier of the infinite.
    Graceless, the infinite fingers me,
A simulacrum of true woman, even as she
Moves for my pleasure in her half-undress.
    Tormenting me will never do, my friend.
Though you are the infinite, I am human.
I see the fire, in its flames, contend
It would be, were it possible, human.
    So go, you Bastard, fuck off forever,
And leave me writing in this clement weather.

IN PRAISE OF PERIGORD

Douce land of grass and golden stone,
    Wide rivers, where the limestone caves
Reveal how hand of man alone
    Redeems how mind of man behaves,

Your forests, maize, tobacco, yield
Ten thousand sunflowers in a field.

We walk your treasury of trees
    Dappled by sunlight so serene
The wood-doves coo us to our ease
    Ensconced in soul-erupting green.
Before us, through your grassy banks,
    Winding like a silver road,
The Dordogne, image of a god,
    Distils our mortal thanks.

Fred Beake

b. 1949 in Cheshire, but brought up in Yorkshire, where he wrote his first poetry when in his first year at Tadcaster Grammar School. He read History at Sussex University, but left without taking a degree. For some years after university he lived near Whitby, then settled in Bath in 1972. Beake published his first pamphlet of poems with Outposts Publications in 1970; a Selected Poems from the University of Salzburg in 1991; and several smaller collections in the years between. He has translated considerably from the French and Latin. A deep interest in the Modernists – especially the Imagists and their heirs – existing side by side with a love of the more formal traditional poets of England has given his work, as Jon Silkin has written, an 'idiosyncratic' twist making him a sort of Spenserian Imagist (eidetic as much as real) whose structural techniques are more often free than formal. As with Bunting, so with Beake, there is an obsessive reaching after complicated and, as yet, unformulated areas of musical experience in language. There is frequently a medievalism, even a hint of the Dark Ages, in his poetry. But there is also a vein of the satirical, often coupled with an historical and patriotic sense. Despite an active involvement in the West Country with provincial poetry groups, the running of a small press, and a sufficiency of poetry publications from his pen over more than twenty years, Beake's work has received little critical attention. The principal reasons for this are almost certainly that his poetry makes insufficient concession to the dominant demotic tradition of the Age of Larkin; too much concession to Modernism and its Post-Modernist successors; and is, as Silkin said, individual to the point of idiosyncrasy. It is work that betrays the fractured sensibility of a poet divided almost exactly between the traditional and the avant garde.

IT WAS ON A DAY OF WHITE FROST

It was on a day of white frost like this that I pranced
        through the fields towards the river.
A robin was perched on the catkins singing.
        There I paused and listened.
I knew this was what I had come for, and not
        the river's shifty hugeness. So I
listened till the frost entered into my feet
        and my nostrils and throat grew too sore
and then returned to where we lived, which even
        now I could take you into each
room of, though it is all of thirty years since
        we left it for a place where the frost
could not craze the windows past the art of man.

SIGNS

The Romans to resolve
their death-grapple with Hannibal

sent a fair part of their cabinet
half the known world

to fetch a chancy god
from Asia Minor

When I was pruning
the Reverend Goodman's apple trees

nostalgic for a love
that shall not be repeated

an apple on a twig
brushed me with new beginnings

Somewhere beyond hopelessness
the two connect

I CAME TO THIS CAFE

I came to this cafe
nearly twenty years gone
cycling out of Bath
the steep and dusty road
in the windless sweat
of a hot summer
a young boy
weather bronzed
in tee-shirt disrespectable
baggy grey shorts
following out of the north
a rumour of ancestry
and failing
after the manner of boys
set by adults
to an adult task
and now I return in spring
two lovers wiser
two children younger
sadder less prone to anger
pondering on all this
and diverting
my thoughts to Artorius
in a time
like his
of slipping foundations.

FOR MY BROTHER IN A DARK TIME

The Godsmith of Nihil
is at the atom's core.

How should we cry against the evil
that buds in ourselves?

My brother would climb the damson tree

towards the mothering sky

and gather the purple fruit
with joy, but his jokes

were of the shitten earth
and now his mind has broken.

Teach me in these days of uncaring
to bend like the wheat in the wind

and turn away from me such gales
as beat even wheat to the ground.

A BALLAD

She loved me for an hour
of untrampled ecstasy,
But then she turned to another
and I was lonely.

But then she came knocking at my door,
and between her thighs was growth,
And we grew two trees in one tree,
and our buds were more than death.

But the abrupt angers of the Spring
passed on to summer calms,
And the lees of the summer was bitter,
but the unleaving of Autumn worse.

And in the frosts of the Winter
our trees split apart,
And part of me is living
and buds both green and bright.

But I know in the heart of me
this dream grows darker,

And only the faith of a true lover
can ever make it lighter.

So arise my moon – my fertility –
my sun of all energy,
And cry my winds from infinity.
Let me again begin to be.

Anne Beresford

b. 1929 in Surrey; educated privately, and at Central School of Speech and Drama; stage actress, broadcaster, and drama teacher. In a line from a poem of hers 'even in laughter the heart finds sadness', I sense the essence of all this poet's judgement on life. Years ago, reviewing her volume *The Curving Shore* (Agenda Editions) I put it thus: 'A nostalgia of disenchantment like an invisible mist exudes from many of Anne Beresford's poems. Each is clearly angled as a sharp sigh.' Dennis O'Driscoll says much the same thing more bluntly: 'From the start, Anne Beresford has taken a dim view of the world, her dominant vision pessimistic and bleak. But her response has been controlled rather than petulant...' So why bother to write poetry? Because, like H.D., Anne Beresford sees fragments of beauty everywhere. So why the critical neglect of her beyond the pages of *Agenda* magazine, her publisher and supporter these many years? It may be that she has been too closely associated with that distinguished periodical – a situation which, less-than-charitable murmurings have suggested, can sometimes prove counter-productive, leading, for example, to charges of exclusivity. The opposite effect, in fact, of being too widely published in many magazines. It may, in addition, be that – in their hearts – most readers and critics cannot take a pessimistic world-view. Such was held against Hardy for a century, and restricted the fuller appreciation of his poetry until quite recently. It may be that Beresford overworked a commitment to Imagism and the free line, and got left behind by more metrically-demanding times, at least in the UK. One cannot be sure, but I am certain that Anne Beresford is one of beauty's exiles in an ugly age; and that has somewhat wrong-footed her work critically.

DISTANCE

We were friends years ago –
walking to school along respectable streets,
touching, smelling all that suburbs have to offer.
We shared friends the same way we shared sweets.
Sometimes we quarrelled.
London kept us slightly distant.

In the country we had a deeper communion.
For hours we sat by streams, silent,
to hear the gurgling of water
on stones and dried leaves.
We lay, on sunny days, among thyme and rosemary.
Stole redcurrants, which hung,
like an Aunt's necklace, on green threads.

The antics of adults puzzled us.
Fascinated we watched them balancing
tea cups on floral knees,
sprinkling fruit cakes with sugar,
downing whisky or dabbing perfume.
Idle days. We learnt much.
Not enough. Our years stretched unending.
We looked forward to growing. To freedom.

Back in town we played with dolls.
Witnessed mysteries and anguish we had no part in.
Went to church, over the common where seagulls
shrieked above the pond.
We discovered later that hell yawned beneath us.

Our respectable streets shook with bombs.
It was about then – when the safety
of childhood was crumbling –
we began to part company.
A slow process. One night,
after she'd screamed out her grief
at the minor cruelties of life –
the rows, smell of whisky and vomit –
she withdrew. To a world of dreams

I thought. But perhaps I was wrong.

In any case we lost touch.
Forgot her – almost. Until this morning
I opened a book and saw her name written
clearly, in a childish hand –
and a photograph. A thin child.
Nothing remarkable. Missed her suddenly.
Remembered scrambling over rocks
looking for shells, scampering over the moors
to pick heather. Nothing remarkable.

Shut the book, and wrote on a scrap of paper:
wish you were here.

DECEMBER

It was towards evening
he walked out of the sun
he could've been a pilgrim.
The dogs didn't bark
as he lifted the latch of the gate.
He said he was going home
pointing to the mountains.
He asked for water.

Now the trees sway
in the east wind
the mornings frosty
snow on the hills.
I keep thinking
how his eyes searched
and smiled
his hand delicate
on the cup of freshly
drawn water.

And I think

as I stir the fire
or peel potatoes
how there have only been one or two
illuminated moments
in my life
the rest is as nothing.

RAIN

Rain drips
from broken gutters
drips through the roof
through the ceiling
through any crack it happens to find

on the lawn
a pheasant tried to hide its head
the feathers heavy

The woman
moves from room to room
places a bucket
to catch the leaks
stares at the blotted sky

then
takes up her thoughts
where she had left them

"It matters little
that so-called time
races onwards or fills the day
with worries and trivialities...

the first apple tasted bitter
bitter and new...
we were all new...
agape, love

those words came later
in God's old age"

Heather Buck

b. 1926; a poet of the realms of introspection and the fragile intellect, who began to write in her forties as a result of Jungian analysis. Her poetry testifies, in its quiet way, to the awful and awesome struggle for mental health that afflicts so many in the modern world, that overcoming 'of the empty space':

> ...until from the vast
> open canvas of nothing, something climbs
> over the mind's horizon, settles
> into the yawning hole of my boredom,
> and I wake to the revelation
> of its ordinary everyday shape
> and the magic of life as it is.

This is a quiescent poetry, yet one that confronts honestly that which induces breakdown in many minds. It is Emily Brontë minus the sad rhetoric, the music; but which still reveals all those little beauties and big sadnesses in suffering. Lastly, it is quasi-religious poetry: one often metaphysically reaching after a teleology in life. Because Heather Buck's style is not mannered, not slangy, not cynical nor outrageous, however, her books seem to have passed by more quietly than even Edith Scovell's or Ann Riddler's. I can't say exactly why, except perhaps that her poetry is too elusively metaphysical – neither denominationally religious, nor frankly aesthetical – for contemporary taste? Whatever, despite a good publisher in Anvil Press, she hasn't qualified for the flash anthologies which tell us what the trends of the time are. But, then, there are other forms of wisdom...

MOVING HOUSE

Like a life that dies on a summer's afternoon,
The blood in the veins of the house
Is weakening now. Was strong and thick
In the arteries, and livelier still
In the children's songs.
The inquisitive sun is sprinkling light
On the chairs, the tables, the cups and plates,
And the strange black van that is waiting.

There were doors in the house that opened
Only at times, for the keys were lost.
But the other doors swung on their hinges
And the rooms became worn to the shape
Of the lives that fitted them.

There were faces that came out of the mist
Surrounding us, stayed for a time,
Now are dissolved in the cherry tree's flowering,
Or preserved in a dream that recurs.

Now the rooms are all disordered by emptiness,
Sudden exposure of dust, and paint that is peeling.
In the drive an armchair sags in the sunlight,
And holly and yew are sheltering things
Like displaced persons, all huddled and bruised
Waiting their next rough handling.

EPIPHANY

We discover that where we
are is where we belong.
Thomas Merton

There's an absence always there, like
an ache in the gum the probing tongue
won't leave alone. In the hungry void
of an unfilled Sunday I see them as shadows

through glass, endlessly walking
backwards and forwards, and I haul the comfort
of Monday's tight schedule towards me.

As they pave the unseen abyss with laughter
I'm tempted to envy, but I've walked
other pavements trying to fill
the mind's empty basket; wrung the text
of promising books dry as squeezed lemons,
and found myself stranded high on a beach
while the shouts of bathers
boomeranged over the hot white sand.

So I sit it out, the nagging pain
of the empty space, the lack of distraction;
resist the cheap book or film that sucks in
the whole afternoon, the easy options
of chatter and drink, until from the vast
open canvas of nothing, something climbs
over the mind's horizon, settles
into the yawning hole of my boredom,
and I wake to the revelation
of its ordinary everyday shape
and the magic of life as it is.

THINGS

Let me not use you fig, fruit, flower,
let me not gather others to admire
my part in your accomplished hour, and though
it take a lifetime to forfeit all desire
for this moment I rejoice, simply that you are.

Let me not cast my shadow over things,
nor let my failures cloud their shapes
when forgetful of their permanence
I strut and preen on life's precarious stage.

Things will not notice when I die
for measured by rock, stone, sky,
I am a firefly quick against the night,
a particle that slipped creation's swollen sack.

Enough to have been here, to have come upon
a blaze of sunflowers jostled by the sun,
to have seen beyond the rack of self
Mont Sainte Victoire painted by Cezanne.

REMEMBRANCE DAY PARADE

The bugles mourn across the cold bright day,
of all the evocations of our pain
that most articulate.
Unfallen leaves are blown through trees,
the iron fence crumples them in heaps,
and we turn hurriedly
from all those wheelchair citizens
who sit upon the sidelines of our lives
and watch our greed and self-indulgence grow
like festering sores upon their broken limbs.

Their anger breaks about us like a shower of hail,
it makes no odds, we wear
our self-absorption like chain-mail.
But when they turn their wheelchairs
towards their life apart,
to where the sun slants
through the tall institutional quiet,
these, the privileged who survived
still paste and wire mementos
of the poppy-fields of France.

Douglas Clark

b. 1942 in Darlington, County Durham, of Scots parents. Studied mathematics at Glasgow University and Edinburgh. One of those Scots whom, in earlier times, the English Imperial Adventure would have carried farther afield than Bath, where he has lived for the past twenty years or more, having 'found contentment in the magical world of computers'. A true eccentric, he burst upon the world in the 1980s entirely unnoticed, with *five* substantial self-published volumes of poetry. Well, not entirely unnoticed, for *Stand* described Clark as 'an amateur in the best sense'. Just as the Goths came from nowhere and civilised Europe in their shadowy, mysterious way (and just as the Men of Arthur have always remained shadowy), so there is something both mildly modern gothic about the emergence of Clark's poems and their style: a 'processional headed by a black-robed cowl' – and something mythopoeic, too. But as the procession has proceeded, Clark has more and more made his voice heard, and shown his wide range of concern, from the delightful homely *Fritz Cat* poems, to his deeper historical preoccupations as in the marvellously panoramic poem called *The Mong* about the Mongolian conquests of Asia. At their best his more personal poems, no matter their ostensible subject, afford us a glimpse of a retiring bachelor figure living out his life quietly in Bath, obsessed by mathematics, myth, and the Muses; and, as *Stand* also said, 'determined to play the game his own way' – which, of course, is no recipe for being noticed. It would be wrong, however, not to point out that self-publication is not only the easiest way into print, it is also the safest way – as a general rule – to *avoid* critical attention.

YOUNG BROCK

I have seen foxes parade down the centre of our streets
Under the sodium lamps,
I have seen and heard hedgehogs scuttle up the path
Outside my house;
But never, until last night, have I been face to face
With mystery.

For sixteen years I have walked home across the green
On returning from the pub,
All I have ever seen on the way have been boisterous dogs
Watched over by nervous owners.
Last night was the different night,
I heard a noise and stopped and stared.

Young Brock was ten yards away,
His white streaks showing on his head.
The night was silence and there were no stars.
We stared at each other for a full minute,
The magician and the badger,
The wisest beings in the world.

Then like a hare he was off down the hill,
So close to the ground.
I hope he has come to keep me company,
It is lonely in solitude with Fritz Cat.
After sixteen years the badgers are come
And I have communion with Lords of Nature.

SEVENTEEN

There was only one way out
Of the hell-hole of fourteen.
That was by being top of the class.
I kept my ambition to myself.
Never revealing it at home.
And I made it.

Then at seventeen I met Cornelius.
He was so much more brilliant than I
That there was no competition.
He was waiting to go to Cambridge.
I competed for a while
But then had to throw in the towel;
Skulk off to Glasgow feeling inferior.
At Glasgow I was top again.
But I had learnt that there are people
In this world whose ability transcends belief.
And I was not of the elect.

TWENTY, THIRTY, FORTY

Twenty four was clean white sheets and Jo,
That was when it came together and fell apart.
When everything was great and natural
But I had someone to meet.

Thirty four was saying goodbye.
The last glimpse of a lost face
Through the shadows of a window.
That was the beginning of a new Hell.

Forty four was Torremolinos and Granada,
The writing pouring out of the heart.
I had no-one to meet
And I had woken out a ten-year trance.

Love's imagination has been my ruin.
I chased after all the rainbows
And found nothing but disillusion.
There is always an empty space to be filled.

Back to the agony of fourteen
Without the magnificent immortal dreams.
I never expected anything from life.
I won't be disappointed.

from LOVE SONNETS

Envy the boy with his girl in the park
So young self assured arrogant intact
He floats in a dream secure that she's there
One twitch of her eye he's walking on air
Look after him girl say all the right lines
Dazzle and dazzle but remember he's blind
Stand straight there before him look in his eye
Give him your picture then you'll live till he dies
Be gentle be kind don't force his young sex
He'll come in good time it's his head that's erect
Tell stories tell magic create him your art
And always before him Oh warm his struck heart
You're so far beyond him but teach him in jest
There's jokes writ in Heaven he'll never regret

PLANTS

I will never stop writing about Coatham Mundeville.
I design the books that will last forever,
And put Susan at the centre.
No woman would want to marry me
As long as she is on the planet.
The only certain thing about Susan is that she will behave badly,
Like a creature out of Jane Austen.
It is rough without you, Susie.
I do the best I can.
Long may you run.

I will never stop writing about Coatham Mundeville.
Yesterday I started work on my garden for this year.
I dug out the twenty-year-old roses,
Ruining my back and gloveless hands.
Today I bought replacement plants and installed them:
White, yellow, pink and red.
Tomorrow I must buy seeds of alyssum, pansies.
I haven't been involved with my garden for fifteen years.

But now in my retirement
It is time to be creative.

I will never stop writing about Coatham Mundeville.
It is better to love than to be loved.
Tell the truth but tell it slant.
I have planted cuttings of my lamb's ear, snow-in-summer,
I hope it was not too cold last night,
It is a time for fertility.
I went out in the morning air
For it was that time of year,
I looked out over my green domain
And said: Death hath no fear.

Jack Clemo

b. 1916; of village school education: 'A poet without nostalgia, without the negative / Kindling of transience and despondency.' Like his fellow Cornishman A.L. Rowse, one of those unique hard-edged, near-reclusive minds which that county produces: the Celtic-Englishman – an extraordinary type – Jack Clemo has not suffered quite the same critical neglect as some poets in this volume. In one way this is surprising, considering his off-putting Calvinism, and his completely unsentimental attitude towards the natural environment, indeed, his positive glee at its destruction:

> Exulting as the refuse spreads:
> 'Praise God the Earth is maimed,
> And there will be no daisies in that field
> Next Spring...'.

Not exactly a fashionable view to hold in an increasingly 'green' century! In another way, however, a Christian 'self-taught English working-class visionary writer', even in a largely post-Christian era, who is a good poet, must especially fascinate. One thinks of the parallel case of R.S. Thomas, a more acclaimed poet than Clemo, but one who continues to receive attention from a (at least nominally) Christian Establishment, and from a wide range of readers and critics who still hanker for some kind of faith in this secular wilderness we all inhabit. All the critical attention in the world, however, could not lessen the sense of exile – of being a 'being apart' – that characterised Clemo (who died as this volume was in preparation), as it did his great predecessor in the nonconformist tradition, John Bunyan, with whom he has frequently been compared. There can be few contemporary poets whose ideas and attitudes are as uncongenial to the modern mind as were Clemo's, yet whose work, especially his earlier, is incontestably inspired.

THE PLUNDERED FUCHSIAS

They lie all round the lawn
And on the furrowed wall
Like little red bombs winged and splayed.
No gale has made them fall:
A child's whim, that is all.

She plucked one from the bough
And squeezed the calyx, nipped
Till up welled honey – one clear drop
'Mid pistil-shafts blue-tipped.
Next moment they were ripped

Greedily out and flung
Across the garden while,
The petals underneath her tongue
Pressed backward, she made trial
Of nectar; then her smile

Lit up; sweet vandal hands
Pillaged more blooms, stripped bare
A whole branch in a wasteful freak.
For once she did not care
That a flower's face could be fair.

In those moments she was mine,
The love of beauty's dress
Dead in her eyes, her fingers numbed
From pity or caress
Of Nature's loveliness.

Dear God, but it was heaven
To see her red lips meet
Those petals with no kiss but glib
Destructive glee, and cheat
The bees of their stored sweet.

She marred the rhythm of soil,
She checked fertility,
And then, the last flower trampled on,

She turned more naughtily
And gave her lips to me.

Alone and trembling I
Stoop now, but not with fear:
These pistils cannot stab my faith:
Each is a limp spear
That withers as I peer.

The flower-shells strewn to die,
Dismantled by her lips,
Were drained where my new life has fed,
The life that only grips
Where Nature's in eclipse.

MOOR HUNT

A dredger at that sour and shabby pool
Like a blood-sucking vampire; that flat heath
Bristling for miles, its massive threat unsoftened
By a hedged road, cottage or cordial tree.

I had known from infancy
That this was Goss Moor, but I feared the place,
Never cheered when my well-meaning uncle
Led me out past the groping dredger,
The choked tarn, to see huntsmen arrive
On an autumn afternoon, hailing from Fowey.

Brightly-clad folk on horses, urging
Lean hounds that sniffed or bayed,
Scenting prey. It seemed all of a piece
With the blood-sucking image by the pool.
I would picture the trapped fox and creep,
Hurt and shaken, back to Penrose farm,
Where a bucket soon clacked in the homely well
And I could relax, ready for the bracing tea.

BEAUTIFIC VISION

Gaunt to the marrow, iron-scarred
As the jail he fled from at Toledo,
The monk John thanked heaven for absolute
Unbroken darkness. A cutting tick of light
Would have betrayed him, and he fancied
An inner parallel.

The soul's disgust with temporal comfort, its taste freed
From festive candles, romantic moon.
John scorned them as carnal flickers
Foiling the escape from self
To the sublime, unrivalled union,
God's clasp of the stripped ascetic.

Did not some wedded Spanish artist
Find a healthier way after baptism
Through the bride's smile, ripe olive-groves in a painting?
He would have known blessed kindlings, the heart's
And high art's vowed frontiers
Heaven-flushed outside the world's prison,
And spirit purged for its last prayer
When farthest from the cloisters.

T.E. LAWRENCE

Just here, in this crabbed Dorset hut,
    Lawrence, you pieced an Arabian saga, heights
Of valour and endurance, but
    Never the sound hearth's comforts, bridal rights.

You loved red barren sand,
    Detesting marriage and St Paul:
Even at your door I cannot understand
    Such a creature's world at all.

I thrive on Pauline toughness, grace at home

In awkward signatures of bliss
When seven or more pillars of crusty wisdom
Crash as a creed transforms a kiss.

There was, of course, the fact
That your birth was illegitimate.
This must be said with tact:
It was, in your day, unfortunate.

You screened the bruise of shame,
Clutched at a harsh material sanctity
Of drilled machines, war flame
And danger's dubious mystery.

Did hints of a broad transcendence
Strike as your motorcycle roared
To the fatal thud? Perhaps the essence
Of our debt to you lies stored

In the track of Homer, your Odyssey,
The tremulous Greek hope
Set ina new candour. Still, this house is empty,
Voiceless to me. I have no taste for a grope.

John Cotton

b. 1925, London. Educated at London University; and was an officer in the Royal Naval Commando, Far East, in World War Two. Subsequently, a teacher with the Middlesex Education Authority, he wound up headmaster of Highfield Comprehensive School, Hemel Hempstead. He edited the poetry magazine *Priapus*, with Ted Walker, from 1962 to 1972; and the journal of fine presses, *The Private Library*, from 1969 to 1979. Ex-chairman, treasurer and general council member of the Poetry Society for over twenty years, he became Deputy Lieutenant of the County of Hertfordshire in 1989. He is the author of many books of poetry and verse, both for adults and children.

There is an element of commonsense at the heart of Cotton's poetics: 'I explore my emotions and attitudes and, of course, the language in which I express them. If I succeed in this it is for others to judge.' Commonsense or not, a great truth is revealed there, for not many poets – because of their almost maternal fixation with their own work – can face up to the fact that it really *is* for 'others to judge'. The modernised nature poet that Edward Marsh wanted to summon into being for his Georgian anthologies was, in ideal terms, someone like John Cotton. Someone thoroughly alive to our heritage and landscape, with a nice line in nostalgia (not sentimentality), yet absolutely aware of, and reflecting, the changes that TV, the cinema, and general Americanisation, have brought about. Someone contemporary, compassionate, and completely aware of all sides of nature and life, from the beautiful to the bad; and with the sort of ear that can produce a language in poetry that is neither aureate of diction nor excruciatingly demotic, but plainly and truthfully unaffected. Not the sort of poet to have got into the neat, gentlemanly *England's Parnassus*, nor the philistine realism of the Bloodaxe *New Poetry*, but a poet like John Heath-Stubbs, humorous without straining to play the funny man, a poet who can give you sex without any impression of prurience: John Cotton is that man.

TRISTESSE

(The thought of heaven, however doubtful, helps to keep us going)

Warmly buttoned in her winter coat,
She appears to hesitate, to respond?
Between the fur hat and the coat's collar
Her petal cheeks are rouged and powdered
By the frost that hones the air.
Her fresh scent sharp,
And the small clouds of her breath
As sweet as mangoes.
Invulnerably vulnerable,
It is an illusion
She can conjure, quite innocently.
Can you lose what you never had?
She'll make you think so.
A razor slash of regret,
A fine gift, an image,
A fragile haunting.

QUIET

Once there was quiet in the valley,
We could hear the slow thoughts of mountains,
The breathing of small hills,
And at evening the dark forest trees listening to the silence.
Then came traffic
And it was never the same.
The earth stopped hearing
And the still small voices were drowned.
Though sometimes in the early pre-dawn hours
The quiet will pay sly secret visits
From where it waits.

PAST

Because we loved we took the photographs.
They show us people who used to be us.
Small pasteboard souvenirs of affections
That haunt the past like the seed husks
Of the campion in Winter hedgerows,
Small dusty reminders of Summer.
Those passions long dampened now,
Subject only to imagination's resurrections.
Were they as good as that?
Possibly. Who cares, so long as they can bring
Light to chill rain-soaked days
When the clouds' grey brushes that of the sea.

A TOUCH OF FAME

(Eric Gill's Diary March 1915)

I met a famous man once.
He offered me two bob to put his hand up my skirt.
Well times were hard and he seemed harmless enough,
More like a priest in those long robes and that.
He was gentle, and when he slipped his fingers into me
He said it was the nicest one he'd felt for a long time.
I should think so too!
I've always taken the best care of myself I could.
Though I gathered later it could have been a bit of a compliment,
As I learnt that he'd had it
Not only with his wife, his and her sisters,
Cousins, nieces, and a small regiment of servant girls,
But even visiting Fathers who had come to say Mass,
Plus 'experiments' with the family dog!
It was all religious with him it seemed,
Something to do with being close to the sources of creation.
The stories they make up!
I've not told anyone else before,
But it can't be all that many women like me
Who've had such hands in their drawers

As made those lovely letters on the Underground Stations.
Though, thinking about it, I reckon he got the better bargain!

QUARTIER BENAUD

(La Chaise Dieu)

Out there the one street lamp rinses
The cow-pat patinaed road and rough stone walls
With a light in which the shadows come off best.
All is quiet except for the pulses of trees,
The house's small complaints
And the breathing of a darkness pricked with stars.
Dogs are having uneasy dreams of their peers,
One punctuates the night with a metronome of barks.
Awakened we fend off memories of failure
As they ease their way to envelop us.
Morning will bring the chatter of hunch-shouldered martins
Preening before they carve the sky's feast.
Flies are already whinging in the kitchen.
Then the soft-shoe shuffle of the gentle-eyed cows
Who grant as they pass their epiphany
Of a sweet sickly incense of fructifying dung,
While the mellow Abbey bells toll of redemption.

NIGHT

(St Ives)

We look from a window that does not open
Through which the years judge us.
A bead-string of lights outlines the bay,
The motes of headlamps distantly flicker
On a line of land thrust out into the Atlantic.
In the room a row of sepia worthies assesses us:
College groups, the disapprovingly bearded,

Their past frowning on our frivolity.
A drift of music floats out into the dark
Across the pewter moonlit waters,
An ephemeral counterpoint
To the ocean's restless shoulders shrugging,
An erosion that lasts and salts the eye.

Michael Croshaw

b. 1943, Warwickshire; left school at sixteen and did a variety of jobs before settling with British Telecom, taking early retirement from the latter in 1991. An independent, associated with the highly-independent *Orbis* magazine as co-editor for eight years. A non-university man proving perhaps that you have to go to some sort of university these days to 'get anywhere in poetry'? Speaking for myself, the language of successful poetry is the heightened vernacular: the best branch of the common tree of language because the most highly-wrought; but, in his recently published selected poems, *A Harmony Of Lights*, Croshaw admits to the old Wordsworthian hang-up about 'the Parnassian' versus the spoken tongue: 'I see this Parnassian trend as the greatest single flaw in the whole history and development of English poetry'. The dichotomy is a false one: the language of English poetry at its best has never been, and never will be, 'the language spoken by men to men', etc. Surely, the one stream feeds the other? So I am not surprised, when turning to Michael Croshaw's poetry to find it governed by a polish and refinement, a subtlety and skill that is quite outside the scope of the demotic. (Indeed, he is often slightly more 'parnassian' than many of his contemporaries, but we will let that pass.) At his best, Croshaw is a fluent and thoughtful poet, intelligent of message, never trivial, and so well read and versed in the tradition of English poetry as to be capable of the most brilliant parodies. I hope, when the time arrives for his work to be given a fuller critical treatment, the disparity between his theory and practice will be carefully considered, because it will cast some light on his, at times, over-facile talent. Although Croshaw has produced a number of very distinguished poems by any standards, there seems to me to be, at the heart of his poetry, something of a linguistic compromise that may well be traceable to the conflict between his ideas of the Parnassian and the Vernacular.

FRIDAY NIGHT IN THE FISH AND CHIP SHOP

The Browning Version

I slipped on the scallop, and Janis and he;
I tottered, they tottered, we tottered all three.
Splash went the vinegar over the floor!
We fell in a heap, and were joined by some more.
And skinheads, who thought this the cue for a fight,
Threw bottles and ashtrays, and out went the light.

And there in the darkness we groped and we fumbled,
Where Terry and Janis and others had tumbled.
'Stop!' cried the manager, trying to guess
Just who was to blame, through the chaos and mess,
As he grabbed by the collar and arms the fish-frier,
Who was doing his utmost to put out the fire.

And those who had managed to get to their feet
Were choking and fighting their way to the street.
I followed, with Janis – perhaps Terry too,
I can't really say – it was all I could do
To keep myself upright. Confusion and smoke
Soon got in the way, and I started to choke.

I fell again. Janis sank down on her knees.
We'd slipped on a carton of faggots and peas,
Surrounded by screaming, uproarious boys
Who were fighting and fencing with huge saveloys.
I, Janis and Terry gave way to despair
As the hard pickled onions sailed down through the air.

And that was the scene when the officers came,
The police, and the firemen to put out the flame.
And to the police station went Terry and I
(They let Janis go, but they didn't say why),
And he and I told them, amid sound and fury,
About our involvement. They smiled at the story

And said they'd be contacting Terry and me,
As we poured down our throats their undrinkable tea.
They let us go home under grey morning skies

To bandage our wounds and to nurse blackened eyes,
And that is the reason I, Terry and she
Stay home Friday evenings and watch the tv.

THE MADONNAS

Out of the mouths of all the madonnas of the world
flows the sweet breath of the seasoned blood of Christ,
like a lily in Hebron,
like an Easter of sighs and muted laments.

As from the tall candles of Christ's munificence
sings the white empire of the dove's mountain dream
like summer's kiss to the children of darkness and winter,
like the warm carolling of soft-covering hymns,

so, in the smiles of the madonnas, reposes daybreak
and mystery of dawn's cool annunciation,
stations of sweet crossfire of eternal flame,
immutable mandala of endlessness.

And when the madonnas spread hands of rain and manna
over the parched, starved lands whose thirsty springs
are the Ezekiel bones of a dry dead letter
rasped from the world's mouth by unyielding famines,

killing word and spirit with serpent-hiss
sure as sapless bodies that bleach in the sun –
from the mouths of the madonnas falls, like fine bread,
releasing symbol, Logos of everlasting.

Oh the madonnas are white barley mothers
guarding offspring like grain in a blight-bright noon:
yes, the madonnas are light, unchained air
beyond the dungeon capsule of the soul's gloom.

And to them, as the fears of trembling children
speed for relief to a mother's calling arms,

tears and alarms of the world cry from a wilderness
beyond love's embrace for succouring balms.

LADIES

Wrapping their parcels of land in gracious smiles,
they raised parasols
at sporting teas, regattas, fairs and fêtes,
noblesse oblige falling from them like rain
upon the ranks beneath:
gardeners whipping support for racing whippets;
unstable stableboys loitering within beer tent;
curtsying parlour maids bashfully 'walking out'
with colliery lads, softly tinkling belles
acting so *humaine* with their sooty *bêtes*.

Now, tiaras pawned, the mounting debts
decosmeticizing their rouged features,
they run horses for courses and open their doors
to everyone, conducting through galleries
enshrined to a varnished age the holiday trippers.
The old veneer gone like the sold Vermeer,
they sell instant past to the careless child
who leaves fingerprints on Morris wallpaper
and marks of muddy feet on de Morgan tile.
They stay as exemplars and history teachers,
and marriages, less stylish than before,
are mortgaged to social change. As dinner guests,
proposers of toasts, they still shine briefly feudal,
but otherwise, apart, anachronistic,
they live in a limbo of moon and madrigal
as, from the church hall once so deferent,
a different sound is heard on Saturday night,
the howl of defiant youth at the discothèque.

SPRING AT CANNON HILL

Once more the windmill laughs.
The Arts Centre waves a subsidised greeting.
It's goodbye winter, farewell ice and epitaphs.
On the grass the birds hop, liberated
from snow-chains. And the sky, the young sky
tremulous as a débutante,
serves its spring novitiate.

Now, renewed, the soft earth underfoot
caresses lovers' feet as they pass bright
and confident, serene with shared future
and ice cream from the banal-voiced, busy van.

Dogs run to the water to bark at ducks.
Boats are busy again. The children's slide
is silver in the sun for Whitsuntide.

Joy, innocence: again we believe in them,
now the winter Rubicon is crossed,
and we dead are awake once more and whole.
No cloudy mansion houses the strong soul
that would brave so much for the smell, the feel of spring.
There's sweetness in the air to relish still
when spring, the green child, sings at Cannon Hill.

Peter Dale

b. 1938; educated at Strode's School and St. Peter's College, Oxford. A teacher at various schools, most recently Head of English at Hinchley Wood School, Esher. Co-editor, with William Cookson, of the literary magazine *Agenda*, he also had connections with the influential *The Review*. His poetry publishers have included Fantasy Press, Macmillan's, Hippopotamus Press, and Agenda. One publisher said of him: 'The trouble with Dale is that he is too critical for the Establishment to absorb him'. In an essay on his work I wrote: 'Peter Dale entirely eschewed the seductions of, and problems posed by, *vers libre*, not by ignoring it and continuing on with the creaking machinery of traditional forms (with all its risk of hackneyed diction), but through, in effect, annihilating open form and the need for it by embracing minimalism'. A consummate craftsman of closed forms – especially involving rhyme – Peter Dale has stubbornly gone his own way over the years, and despite being regarded by many as one of the 'Agenda people', Dale has been entirely true to his art, showing that interest in technique which Pound claimed was the true 'test of sincerity'. Consequently, there are obviously complex reasons for his marginalisation from the contemporary mainstream and its tributaries of fashion. I would hazard that, as with, say, Anna Adams, a devotion to rhyme and metre; plus his inability to endorse the fashionable; and – more surprising it may be thought – Dale's undeniable gift (like Hardy's) for arousing feelings of erotic melancholy, even intimacy, in a highly charged yet formal manner of writing (no dithyrambic outpourings his), have proved obstacles to a just assessment of his work. It is almost as if a special critically sensitive and technically-aware era is needed to do justice to Dale's work – an age of greater refinement than ours perhaps?

MINUTIAE

A petal of compacted mist,
you turn it in your hand,
my old miniaturist.
I shall never understand,
even in crisis, your openness
to moments of small delight;
unyielding, your hands caress
the porcelain, scalloped, white.

– So much of our time gone.
How I am watching you;
love, I am hanging on
that tinge of venous blue
where your inner wrist shows white,
and the porcelain gathers light.

GIFTS

The thoughts I have I cannot give.
    I hardly bear them well myself.
Gifts of my hands I'd like to give
    and tell we share them here and now.

What the gift gives is what I'd give –
    behind this dumb, so yellow bloom...
I'd like to give you happiness,
    the cat that seldom comes when called.

WILL

I'm an old man, shan't waste a word.
Never had much idea of the world;
and the one wish I had for you

never would have been much use.

I wish you liked books. Even my own
fool of a father used to hope
I'd love 'the good book'. (I went
over the top on that as well!)

Most of my life is somewhere in a book;
more than anyone speaks, unboozed.
And mine went there, the whole shoot,
if you want to know me – not that you should.

Or could. Find me there when I'm dead,
in half a dozen books on a desk.
I'll be safe to know then, riffled,
as willows slide light into the river.

And the melancholy long shadows
will lean across the flickering shallows
and you may learn as the light lowers
only the dead heart is not alone.

LULLABY

Sleep, love, go to sleep
and I'll watch over you
as I have done these years,
these shadows of curtain haze,
and breathe into your hair
the things we do not say.

You murmur as if you hear
some saying of the day,
and nuzzle the pillow down
but tracing an edge of light
along your shoulder line
my hands touch on your dream.

A TIME TO SPEAK…

I wanted to say much more than this.
But at the time with all the talk
I couldn't think how best to speak.

The time of our life in front of us,
but I misjudged how long it took
weighing the moment I should pick.

You'd run, I thought, towards me, torn
to utter that long-building cry
half gathered through your idioms.

I've been too quiet. You didn't turn,
but like a wild bird wintering came
to me… and I have given you crumbs.

– Is it bearable snow? Don't leave.
Don't go… This waiting has been love.

COASTWISE

We walked by rivers, dreaming of seas.
– On scarps we peered for other lands;
pitied the poor seagulls without hands –
who went and juggled with the breeze…

– 'Let's not go home until the waves
stop for the night, daddy.'… The shore
was easy walking, years before.
But you'd reject what memory saves.

Yet I would tell you if I could.
I only know the way I've gone.
It's not the way to set you on.
Hindsight may show you where I stood:

The waves edge up; grubby white paws,
and belly-crawl the pebble fringe,
a chidden mongrel in its cringe.
Scutter of stones and shuffling claws.

Peter Dent

b.1938 in Forest Gate, London; has been a schoolteacher for many years, first in Surrey, then in Devon. His poetic sensibility is exceptionally delicate, fastidious and precise: if glassblowers made poems they'd be like Dent's. An early pamphlet like *Proxima Centauri* betrays affinities with that Sixties' minimalism developed by some of the poets around Ian Hamilton's *The Review*; and his handling of the more personal, autobiographical poem has similarities to that of the work of Peter Dale, except that Dent seems to have worked exclusively in free form, whereas Dale has tended in the opposite direction. Reviewing Dent's 1980 collection *Distant Lamps*, Dick Davis captured the essence of his style: 'He has the virtues of the best imagist poets – clarity, *a becoming modesty before experience*, a passion for precision' (my italics); but not necessarily of his technique: 'his verse is never doctrinaire in its technical allegiances', for I feel that his unswerving allegiance to free verse *is* doctrinaire. I believe that for an author to get at what Davis calls in the same piece 'the truth of his subjects' most fully, then music – and therefore metre – must always be an available option. Nevertheless, that said, there are many delights to be found in the work of this butterfly among poets.

WINDOWS

She sidles into view as headlights
swing decisively
to play across an empty drive.

Against the curtain's russet folds
her red dress gleams. Just these,
no other colours to the block.

We watch her fingertips track slowly
down from cheek to thigh,
the sideways glance she seems to fix.

Are we the ones? Dark images
well up again, assert
themselves. Tonight there's no relief.

The bus moves on, accelerating
into rain, but one last
sweeping turn's enough to catch her

in a hail of light. Alone,
no shelter in the restless mind,
she'll take the brunt of night.

RECOGNITION

Careering down the street, a frown
against the noise that presses in.
The coat you wear, too old and heavy,
swinging wildly in your haste...
A sideways glance. You fail to catch
my wave, my call. Predictably.
And while the traffic intervenes,
you disappear.
                    Months since you went
your way alone. Planned meetings out,

now this. Last chance to make amends
as we shall find – your death to weigh
on others too. Cold recognition,
when it comes, will come too late
to cure. The world is out of bounds
too soon. On your side of the street,
where time meets up with some who dare,
I might have checked you with a word.

COLLEGE WITHDRAWAL

The file I want comes easily to hand.
Red lines cut through a name: *withdrawn.*
I skim its papers in the office quiet:
certificates that offer 'nervous state'
while shaky writing in the student's hand
maintains its hurt: 'I ought to leave...'

It's dusk outside, the rain will not relent;
my lamp highlighting death and breakdown,
the child inspired to run away.
Processes, eventualities...
The clerks all know the score and count the hours,
work out their chances for the year ahead.

It's five o'clock. I can't stop now.
Another file unclipped and more to come.
My head is packed with failing lives,
their silent, spinning voices. Pure disorder.
I use the standard forms, meet their demand,
my fingers trespassing in words and dust.

ARC, 1945

Echoing chines and barbed-wire barricades.
She scours the dunes somewhere,
dark glasses hiding eyes. The First War
and her only lover with her still,
his mind shell-bright and gone.

Unseen in distant crevices,
the gunners open up, their target ribbon
half a sky behind the plane. Flash
after flash. No, nothing now is real.
Words make the Channel wider still.

My first time here, her home almost,
where bullets arc through sea-sweet air
and white plumes dance on water.
I climb and cling on to a shattered pine
that lifts me high.

Wide-eyed, I take the whole scene in –
a child, but not alone. Fresh generations
note the red silk scarf she waves,
how fine words travel out
across the air and die

as huge seas pound the beach.

FIRST THING

Slack tide, a window open to the sun
and distance. A little time to kill,
while old objectives gather on the shore.
Here, in the aftermath of dreams, the cold air
dithers at the sill and white gulls drowse.
From first light on, the broken sequences
declare themselves, inviolate histories
we recognise, half-learned and lost.

From roof to lichened roof run sagging lines,
this way and that, the words for ever
in repair. Yet how they shine, as curves
of moisture ring a lover's throat.
Come home, the sky is clear. No wonder
in the onshore wind, the full-blown day.
We're here for moments, odd lacunae where
the colours fall and fold their wings.

Feyyaz Fergar

b. 1919 in Istanbul, and educated by French Jesuits. A famous writer of short stories and poems in Turkey, Fergar's first published book in England was from the neo-romantic Grey Walls Press in the 1940s and was written in French. In 1991 a selection of his English poems entitled *A Talent For Shrouds* appeared from Rockingham Press. Written by and large in free form, these poems are quintessentially poems of gesture and image. Their rhythmic life depends on a persistent gesture of spirit which runs through all of them: a gesture whose effect is to verbally characterise and constantly surprise by turn of phrase, striking image, and subtle thought. Above all he had that rarest of gifts – given to only D.H. Lawrence and one or two other devotees of open forms – of knowing exactly when to end a line. Feyyaz Fergar was a hermetic poet who nevertheless wrote with great clarity; he grew out of surrealism, that last definable stage of Romanticism. How is it then that this man published so little and so late? There is no easy answer to the question. But as a Turk exiled in England who, after the War, became a naturalised British subject, this situation – a yet further variant of the principle of exile – must have played a part. I am reminded of Erich Fried the Austrian poet who lived for most of his creative life in London: he also published little in English, though because of the strong political dimension to what he did publish – something Fergar rejected in his own writing – Fried was somewhat less critically ignored than the Turkish poet. It is profoundly saddening to think that Feyyaz Fergar was just beginning to escape the cocoon of being a foreigner exiled in Britain – was just starting to attract serious attention for his work in England – when he died in 1992. In an odd sort of way, though, the fact that the several obituaries in major national newspapers in this country – which constituted the first really serious treatment of him as a poet in English – formed a sort of testament to his exiled status, not only *away* from Turkey, but also *in* Britain: for how else account for the sudden, if late, rush of awareness? A few editors, of course, had already made public their awareness of Fergar's work in small press journals, but they were in a minority.

WORDS ARE ANCESTORS

What do you mean by "look for the bright side of words"?
What else have we been doing in and out of eras
And down the gutters of time?
Words have not been given to us
To subsidise the monoglot dark and the conservative shore,
They have ways of coming to us, not as semantic skivvies,
But from the deep prows of prodding language,
The strength of horizons in their bones.

Words are at their best when needed to open things
Not to weigh on our tongues like corpses.
They teach houses to spell new doors,
Not to huddle over hoarded rooms.

Refusing the chores of mercenary proverbs
And their coagulant wisdom,
Ready at the height of their breath
To bring alchemy back to its senses
In the crucible of inhaled bread,
Argonauts from roots to sails
Words rise fresh as ancestors on the tree of our eyes.

Hold them up, touch them
If your hands are not forgeries.

TESTAMENT

for David Perman

There is no bad blood between death and me.
He can lay claim to my perishable goods,
my dust, my mistakes, my birthdays.

But when I die I shall leave behind
all the tools of my breath.
I shall leave behind
my eyes, my hands,

the results of my voice,
the roads that lived in my veins,
my habit of smuggling windows into houses
under stark arrest.
I shall also leave behind
the light that stood by me
against the sarcasms of the dark.

With all these I shall speak
for the sun.
Turn your cemeteries off!
There is more to come.

TRUST

He was not one to allow himself
to be branded with a saviour's
guttural charisma. Humility
was his only freedom.

He had a way of being
in touch with trees,
of sharing with them
the shining gifts of the air.

He never imitated, counted
or questioned their leaves.
He never asked them to do
things they were not meant for,
such as giving way to a hanging's
finishing, jerking touch.

When they spoke together
they brought the best out of the text
of the day. Dispelling with urgent hands
the prowling tides of betrayal.

THE WINDOW

Let us start with small things,
Let us into the memory of the palm of our hand
Draw a window,
Let us open it: to let things in.
For instance
The cool shade of a small tree,
For instance
A fish just in time for the sea,
For instance
The sum of a seed,
A look that serves a purpose,
A child who stands on the tip of our tongue,
The eye of a needle that bewitches an embroidery.

Even if nothing comes in
Let us open the window.
We will have had at least
A bit of fresh air,
A bit of hope.

Is that bad?

THE STREET

You have heard it:
this street is now free
for all to cross
or to stroll along.

Do you mean all of us?
the house-to-house executioners,
the merciless angels
of hounding pounding gods,
market-research canvassers
and the devil
in all of us?

Yes.
It takes all sorts
to bring a real street
into being.

To achieve comprehensiveness
we may have to throw in
a couple of stretcher-bearers
carrying a photocopy of the Unknown Soldier
and erect on the pavement
a confessional in the shape
of a curtained telephone kiosk.

VANITY

I must start again,
this is no good at all.
I must sling the fineries
of complexity out of this poem.
Rome and all the roads leading to Rome
are burning and I want to
fiddle with complexities.
Doomtime is upon us and I want
to tart up this sonnet or that strophe
with the baubles of intricate conceit.

Oh no, these words are too heavy,
this is the reign of the thin ice.
Tomorrow I must go and burn
another dictionary.

Geoffrey Godbert

b. 1937 in Lancashire; Geoffrey Godbert has haunted the peripheries of both recognition and the literary metropolis for many years. A friend of Harold Pinter and Anthony Astbury, with whom he has shared the running of the Greville Press, and an admirer of W.S. Graham and George Barker to the point of discipleship, Godbert is not, at first sight, any sort of exile or outsider. Yet one may move among the glitterati, be a guest of the best coteries, and still be an outsider of sorts. Also, self-effacement may lead to neglect; and promoting too much of the work of others (and Godbert has certainly done this through the Greville Press, his magazine *Only Poetry*, and via his own publishing imprint The Diamond Press) may have led to the overshadowing of his own work. Less commendably, from the point of view of the written word, a too-great immersion in the transient world of the transient word, namely in 'performance poetry', can affect the quality of one's work; though in Godbert's case this last has not quite happened, because he has taken as his models the modern Russian masters: the only group which, as a whole, has managed to consistently marry serious verse and the public platform. Despite being the *eminence gris* of the Angles Of Fire performance group, Godbert's poetry stands up better on the page than almost any performance poet I know. Adept at all those rhetorical tricks needed to please a purely listening audience, Geoffrey Godbert has not confined his skills to the trivial and ephemeral. Having read and learned from the likes of Eliot, Essenin and Akhmatova, he has applied his skills to that deep stratum of experience which, when sublimated, leads to genuine poetry.

NOTHING

Saturday night, nowhere to go.
The phone rings in my ear like this:
an owl hooting its engaged tone.
The answer sounds on the silence.
Contact is not made now, nor then:
the pulled-out corkscrew in the cork
pulled out a thousand smiles ago,
the celebration speechless sky,
only the dumb-grey dawn to come.

Saturday night, nothing to do.
Expressively extended, my
annihilating fist screws this
Gershwin memory of mine dry:
can you take this away from me?
The song of it brought rejoicing,
its loss akin to lunacy,
to counting spaces round the words
like sheep incapable of noise.

Saturday night, no one to see.
I am dreaming a long time ago,
the picture just out of focus.
Will they miss me when I'm gone?
The echo is flat as a tongue.
Only a shadow follows me
following the shadows of them.
What happens when the light's turned on?
That is love on Saturday night.

BECOMING

For Susan

You catch me, as it were, with nowhere to go,
while first loves race across the sky like birds.
Poised between a cigarette and a drink

are the confessions and then the tears,
a baby feeling as small as a hand.
Everyone is right about each other:
you have to put your head gently down and rest
and hope the wild-eyed stare will go away,
the sharp pain in a heart will end and that
the edge of living remains.

We must have been in paradise once
to know what it feels like to be expelled, and
do I enjoy a good talk with myself, you ask,
now there are no heroes or heroines left?
Being no one causes you to smile,
becoming eternal costs no one anything.
We are as close as a touch on an arm,
and the arms, you say, taking mine, are linking up.

LASCIVIOUS AUBREY BEARDSLEY, ONLY 25

He uncovered the soft belly of a generation
when he became the first of the nasties
and unfairly loosed impotence on polite fecundity
and made ironic pain out of haughty peace.

His disease gasped down the pretty seaside air
and elegantly vomited chocolate decorations,
fat menopause women, angry embryos
and effete naked gentlemen.

One can think of Beardsley scourged
by wailing earthly monks for dancing
with a 17-stone tart on Brighton beach
(did she pull young Beardsley's trousers down?

and continue to warm her hands salaciously
on Beardsley's iniquitous bottom?)
Truer to remember his drawing from fastidious blots,
mostly of blood coughed up,

his rosebud lips withered, his legs bowed,
his teeth dropped out one by one:
he was as much female dwarf as Salomé.
Though his privacy was pulled up tight like a window,

the glass shaded by a midnight veil,
even Beardlsey could not draw a picture with a flower,
nor perfume normalcy with his exhatations;
and the noxious drip drip of being beautiful

only served to snare his precocious virginity
from the half-life Beardsley drooling over a sin.
He was too much a victim to love visibly;
his held-up crucifix was probably one more promiscuity.

AT THIS LAST TIME OF DAY

At this last time of day
when flowers lower their heads,
bees rest and tears dry

we can still take sleep gently
by the hand and softly
turn like lovers on our backs

and dream such dreams
we have to close our eyes
in order to be able to see.

IN PICTURES

For Danny Milne

In pictures by the Old Masters
the Madonna does not gaze
at her baby, nor he at her.
Both their lives look outward to us;
they gaze on us like eternity.

To us, they are images,
these madonnas, their babies;
they have a love which is worshipped.
In pictures by the Old Masters,
they have that unbreakable beauty.

They pass on their ideal love
which cannot be broken
over the dreadful space
that divides us from them.
It is as if their pictures yearned.

It is as if you yearned for them,
reaching towards their intimacy,
over the paint to their soul;
you stretch out a human hand,
then withdraw; you caress the air.

I WANT TO BE YOUNG AGAIN

I want to be young again,
for in my age is the rage,
knowing, fear: of vertigo,
of water, of speed, of body.
My body has always been
see-through, a soul;
it has lived for centuries.
Now it is forced to live
as though it had never

been alive: why? and why
has it only seconds left?

WE ARE UPSTAIRS TONIGHT

We are upstairs tonight;
upstairs is lovely:
it is wrapped in we.
The poets are downstairs
kissing it goodnight,
staring up at you, me,
their legs fidgeting,
crossing, re-crossing a knee.

Robert Greacen

b. 1920 Derry; brought up in Belfast, but has spent most of his life in London, living at one time with his wife in Ezra Pound's old flat in Kensington Church Walk; now retired to Dublin. Depending on what view one takes of the relationship between Ulster – or indeed Eire – and the British mainland, Greacen's life in London, like that of innumerable Irish, constitutes an especial sort of exile. It is the exile that Yeats knew, and which is well described in Vernon Watkins' poem on Yeats, the sort of exile which a poet needs to find his own voice and discover his own language:

> When I first went to London
> I was looking for technique.
> I had the folk behind me,
> My food was there to seek
> But without the subtlety London taught
> I could not learn to speak.

Other Irish writers – Beckett and Joyce for example – chose exile also, but beyond the English language catchment area, enabling them to develop an almost virtuoso view of their 'native tongue'. But with Greacen, what is 'said' has always been as important as 'the way of saying it'; and I think it fair to claim that Greacen is probably the most 'English' of Irish poets since Louis MacNeice – himself an Ulsterman too. Best known for his charming 'Captain Fox' verse-portraits, there is a directness of treatment of subject coupled with a quiet but noticeable lyricism about Robert Greacen's best poems: the unmistakeable lilt of life. A very human and accessible poet, his Captain Fox is an all-too-British figure which only a foreigner, or an exile, could have created. I have chosen, however, not to include any of them because as a developing 'character sketch' they are better appreciated as a sequence.

THE TRAVELLER

Norton Fitzwarren, Shepton Mallet,
Sheepwash, Black Torrington:
Some such West-country place,
The time a century ago.

An evening black as tar
A knife of wind ice-edged
And never a star to bless the traveller
Nor even cur to argue with snap and bark.
A stranger rode up to the 'Fox and Hounds'.

Inside the oil lamps spluttered
Poured light in saffron pools
Polished the golden cider.
The traveller called for a brandy.
The locals stared, froze into a hush
And crowded round the fire.

No one remembered later how it happened:
A callow youth guffawed, perhaps, to see
A gentleman join the rustic company
Or someone trod upon the stranger's foot
Or spoke a dialect word translated into insult
In the traveller's cold brain.

Putting down his glass he pulled a snake
Out of the pocket underneath his cloak.
"Apologise or die of snakebite," he rasped.
The landlord and the villagers stood agape
Like tableau figures made of wax.
A minute later all had fled
Except for the jelly-bellied landlord.

"Truly I'm sorry sir," he puffed.
The traveller calmly ordered mutton chops,
Drank two quarts of ale and went to bed.

Hours later Jack, an old labourer, died
Of a heart attack brought on by fright,

Young George stayed in bed a whole week
Others screamed in their anguished sleep
So that doctor and parson were hard pressed,
Prescribing and praying for weeks on end.
The greybeards met in council and declared:
"Twas the devil in disguise or we be Dutch."

Then the landlord had a new sign painted,
Renamed his inn "The Snake and Traveller"
And coined a fortune for himself
Not far from Norton Fitzwarren, Shepton Mallet,
Sheepwash, Black Torrington,
Or some such Westward place.

JAMES JOYCE

Now we recall that bitter, dogged Dubliner, James Joyce,
Whose yeasty chaos travelled Europe in his aching brain.
Trieste, Zürich, Paris, Rome and other cities
Knew this young exile buoyed on anger and contempt
For all that was provincial, meanly self-sufficing.
A furnace blazed in his mind's core perpetually
And would not give him rest from constant labour
Until the multi-imaged soul cascaded many thousand words
Barbed and pristine with a febrile, love-hate energy.
Silence, exile, cunning – these sharp keys he cut
To unlock the obdurate gates to Europe,
These keys made in his Dublin prison in friend-wasted days
When Ibsen, Jonson, Hauptmann floodlit each chamber of his mind
And he determined not to honour those fierce claims
Of country, family and church: *I will not serve.*
Then think of him, half-blind and penniless in European towns
Racked by the restive *daemon* of creativeness,
Showing a will inflexible against the little streets
With hatred in their piping, rabble voices,
He ceaselessly dredging an oceanic mind for images
To haunt our splintered century and show us to ourselves,
Crying aloud with all the anguish of our time.

CURSE

Son of a Scots manse though you were
I've taken the rare scunner against you,
You who thieve the golden hours of bairns,
You who bitch up the world's peoples
With dream-like images, coal-black lies,
You who have ended civilised conversation
And dished out licenses to print banknotes,
May your soul shrink to the size of a midge
And never rest in a couthie kirkyaird
But flicker across a million wee screens
And be harassed by TV jingles for ever and ever,
For thine's the kingdom of the *telvisor*,
You damnable bloody genius, John Logie Baird!

THE BIRD

A bird flew tangent-wise to the open window.
His face was a black face of black, unknowing death;
His eyes threw the grim glint of sharpened stones
That children pile by unfrequented roads.

And that night, dreaming into a rapture of cardboard life,
I stared at the lean face of the bird:
A crow I think it was, but it was also death
And sure enough there was the crisp telegram next morning.

I placed my mirror to the flat, unfiltered light
But the razor cut me in spite of the guarantee,
And I knew it was not the razor but the ebony beak
That slashed the base of my left nostril.

I loved the man who lay in the cheap coffin.
It was he first showed me the damp, stereoscopic fields
Of County Down – and now he was away to farm
The curving acres of his jealous God.

I loved the ploughing of his sun-caught brown,
And the hay-lines and the chicken feathers in his hair
That was hay itself, the strongly cobbled boots
And the swaying, coloured idiom of his mind.

And now he was lying with the Holy Bible under his chin,
Sorry only to have died before harvest and turf-cutting,
Lying dead in the room of rafters and the grey, stopped clock –
Because of the hatred of the bird I did not kill.

David H.W. Grubb

b. 1941; Grubb belongs to that generation of poets whose work was fractured by the Sixties' experience with its recrudescence of modernistic experimentalism. Like the somewhat older Ted Hughes – whose hawk was knocked off its rightful perch by an evil crow (something contrary to nature) – Grubb's native poetic talent was shoved off-centre by funny things like late surrealism and the desire to be 'in the swim'. He is a natural English elegist, something of a latter-day George Herbert, but one who has tried to be a Wallace Stevens or a W.S. Graham. This is intended as factual comment not unkind criticism. For Stevens 'the poem' was the 'cry of its occasion', and for Sidney Graham words were their own reality, perhaps the only reality. Grubb's poems are – except when, as frequently happens, family history surfaces to provide 'subject' and to personalise his poems – for the most part as much about themselves as about any reality beyond their own closed self-referential circle. Precisely for this reason – and for a number of people – this makes many of Grubb's poems an important contribution to postmodernism, but I feel this preoccupation to be at variance with his natural talent. It has led – despite widespread publication in the most respected of journals, and frequent collections – to his being yet another 'solitary' on the poetry scene. He needs to be critically challenged in order to get his poetic act more fully together.

DEPARTURES

All of the young years with the old. On dry Saturdays
driving with my father to the old people's home, sitting
in front of those sad smashed-fruit faces with the seconds
collapsing all round us. Everything they said was stolen.
Everything they hoped was dead. The harmonium in the chapel
and the dribbly lips as they sang and the fat one always
wanting to kiss me as we left. As she hugged me I smelt the
loaded sweat and sensed a jolt would pull the sockets out
and let the rusty hair and mossy flesh rub my cheeks.
One of them died one day as we were walking out. She let the
life slip from her like a finished book. I was amazed at the
way the others refused to panic; smiling slowly, offering more sweets.

THE CHURCH IN WINTER

Wind eats stone, yelps snow, hurts God's harsh
bargain against so many faiths.
Few people come here, love or doubt dragging them
back in small congregations
to make this music against oblivion.
The light through old glass seems to have drained
from forgotten seas. Is it God's laughter
we hear in this ruin of rain? Are these His tears?
A simple bell sounds out the loss of years;
a carol for Lazarus or Mozart,
snow crawling against the legends of graves again,
the clock tower telling us things we sense
but cannot believe.

HEDGEHOG

Running down the path like a prickly pie,
the hedgehog has been surprised by the dog
again and dashes away in the rainy day.
The path looks slippery. The weeds bend in
wind like moon grass. The world looks tall
and thin and the only oval shape is the
small, small hedgehog. It looks as if it
will explode at any second. It has a name
given to it by the children. They call it
Mr Lear. The hedgehog knows that this
is silly. It knows its name is really
Harry.

THE DAY OF THE DANCING BEAR

What is important is that they wished to do this
standing in the decorated streets
windows thrown open
a man with a chain and whip and somebody more like
a monkey than a human being
collecting the money in a ragged hat.

The noise must have been tremendous: fat girls biting
into ginger bread and apples
their breasts jumping up like rubber dough when they laugh,
tin pipes and drums and babes held up to see the bear's
brown teeth and freakish grin:
one man holds two dogs, a chicken struts a rooftop as if the
tiles were burning hot: six boys hang out from trees
with eyes like streaks of grease.

The garb of bedlam culminates in what they force
the bear to wear; a bright red jacket with yellow bells,
a dirty feathered hat, pants stretched down to hairy knees:
he scratches at the air with cut-back claws, rips at the faces,
wounds the truth, smashes reality as if its stinks were mortal flesh.

Surrounded by these human wounds
his muscles ape the crooked day;
he knows this will not last but does not mind;
he does not choose to own this joke; beneath a sun of blood
his shadow forms the flames of fame:

the bear is Emperor
in a damaged
land.

TURTLE MYTHOLOGIES

On a shore we cannot reach
turtles begin their journey to another continent
that is essential to the meaning of our history.
They pass midnight swimmers and pleasure boats
and later fishermen whose lights encircle the dependable green.
They pass corals and outer islands and dolphin playgrounds
the ocean gradually becoming dark stars, tiger moons,
far beneath them an endless mosaic of broken bells.
They pass the drowning man's final dreams and the place
where sharks were killed. They pass the immense wreaths
of wrecks. They pass what had been an island village.
They pass the point of recognition, memory, challenge,
identity; intuition pulling them on, the brilliant legend
of their beings giving them energy. They pass from glimmer
of green and shots of silver into deepest grey and gold. They
hear whale song, the nudge of volcanoes, the shift of dunes.
Sometimes, far above them, there is a storm or an iceberg
grates, or a submarine waits with its barbaric store.
Sometimes they have to detour rags of atomic filth,
packages of poison, containers and barrels leaking
death and texts of hate, rags of rage, and ruins of abuse.
Sometimes they have to summon up greater determination
to survive these places, these cruel creeds. In these territories
it would be easy enough to turn back or simply expire, yet
they pass through these passages, they travel on and forget,
they uphold their culture and keep stretching into the

brightness that is waiting beyond them. They are entirely
compelled by the future, the promise of new continents,
the tides of newly becoming, carols of bright beaches
and surging stars, the dawn that must wait for them
and their message, their testimony. Sometimes the intuition of
this becomes so great it rides like waves of stars
and they hear the dolphins urging them on and the green rolls
into gold. Sometimes they hear their ancestors calling them
to become, to create a new world, to enter the meaning
of our history, the planets ordering them to rise and surface.
They pass beyond oceans and lands, surfaces and forms, the
fundamental and the ecstatic, the mission and the meaning,
beyond what had been their purpose, beyond their history,
beyond time and recollection and structure, beyond fusion and
miracle, beyond symbol and data, beyond the God and His
vision, beyond star time and planet pulse, beyond angels
into a map of mythologies.

Harry Guest

b. Wales, 1932, educated at Malvern College, Worcester, Cambridge University, and the Sorbonne. He expressed the poet's sense of exile well in the lines: 'I sit... / brooding on nemesis and fearing / luck... / I write alone and timorous / left contemplating darkness and the sea.' Commenting on his own metrical practice he speaks of using 'syllabics or stress-length lines', with a 'high premium on musicality'. I don't find his work musical, but we'll let that pass; his real strength lies, as Howard Sergeant – his first publisher – observed, in 'skilfully manipulated images and association of ideas'. Guest began publishing his poetry in the 1960s – that decade of confusion in most things, including the craft of verse – and spent six years in Japan, before coming home to immerse himself in teaching in the provinces. The phrases 'a big fish in a little pond', and 'a well-known name in obscurity' spring readily to mind to account in part for Harry Guest's relative neglect, despite regular publication. That, and the following of a rather erratic trajectory in his poetry from the relatively traditional approach in his earliest work, via a period of Sixties' avant gardism, to a reversion to the earlier style in more recent years, with the added bonus that feeling – the essential ingredient of all poetry – has begun to displace the more austere diet of ideas and imagism. There seems to be also, according to the editor of *Acumen* magazine, 'a latent narrative tendency which has yet to fully realise itself in his verse'.

FLORIDA SUNSETS

Gold sprawls above the Gulf, beyond
the cut-outs of palm-trees and low buildings.
The woman filing her tax-return
has to be reminded of its regular display.
A storm sweeping over the keys might raze
each hasty township to flat sand once more.
Who'll gain the ice-box on that quiz-show smeared
with acid green and orange in the corner?
Cars are threaded along the freeway,
three strings of rear-lights, three of yellow.
The sky burns to cinders. Hours
of purchase do not pause. The test
is to summon the novel out of nothingness.
Markets jostle for custom under neon.

No osprey plunges now into the bay.
The citrus colours in the orchard fade.
Tall cypresses, roots clear of stagnant water,
merge into shadow. Spanish moss droops, ghostly,
by a real-estate office open still for trade.
The red rim of evening is lost behind the bridge
and high stars prick a night crisscrossed by 'planes.
Each human effort, sparking, shows, goes out.
Ideas lay down a grid on wilderness
and wander past the swamp, the grass peninsula,
petering out in vacant lots, in dreams
that whisper among waste paper in the dark.

Tampa
Christmas, 1984

A DAUGHTER'S FIRST TERM AT UNIVERSITY

You've said good-bye. She's standing in the car park.
You know there are mallards on that pool in the quadrangle.
A Virginia Creeper sprawls crimson by her balcony.

Later a heron will visit those fields beyond suburbs
but now she has no map to decipher tomorrow,
the clock-face is unyielding, the brochure's out of date, she must
invent a city from scratch and fix names on to strangers.
You know all this. The windscreen-wiper doesn't clear your tears.

'Phone-calls with costs reversed will assure you that certain
seminars are fun, friends have been found. The fact remains –
the one whom you loved as an everyday presence has been
elected citizen of a world you'll never inhabit.
She's left, rightly so, to gain where others have given,
she's cut the cord, packed her bags, embarked on adulthood,
leaving a shadowy stair-well humming with memories
up which you'll clamber trying to tune in to the past.

When she returns, the week-day thrown open in welcome
will lead again to the stunted monolith, the marsh with its orchids.
From time to time you'll stand together on the same
light bridge, high-arched, under which the long-legged
ibises strut with ludicrous, delicate care.
You'll watch with pride the way her hands brush dirt off strange
and gleaming ores. You'll be given fragmentary
and garbled accounts of patterns made, unwoven,
forged again in distant centuries and ivory rooms.
You'll pay attention but she's gone so far you'll never quite
catch up that unfamiliar figure on the changing fields.

THEN AND NOW

for Witold Gracjan Kawalec

She came to kiss her boy good-night.
The shadowed room still buzzed with day:
'I used the grindstone for my knife –
there was a stream of sparks. I helped
pick plums. Oh, the pony threw me –
it didn't hurt a bit – the grass
smelt like vanilla. Anyway
I stuck my stamps in my album till –'

She laid a finger on his lips.
'Hush. Listen to your dreams,' she said.

The air retained her scent. He traced
her footsteps as she went downstairs
though somehow now the house had lost
its walls, a talking bird replaced
the weather-vane, the kitchen-clock
struck seventeen. His sleigh hissed past
high Christmas trees. The snow was warm
as linen. Laughing postmen turned
their letters into butterflies
that flew away above the hedge.

Now I am old and she is dead.
Remembrances before I sleep
cling to the flesh like cobwebs. Night
slams down a coffin-lid and I
might not wake up to prise it off.
Blood pulsing in my head taps out
its own inept Morse code of sour
regrets and grimmer prophecies.
I've lost the knack of listening for
the dreams she wanted me to hear.

WALES RE-VISITED

At home I have had to live as an alien.

The suspension-bridge, grey
rainbow spanning mud and tide,
landed me among the elms of autumn.

I was born on an October cliff
overlooking docks and islands.
Drizzle issued soft from the empty west.
My pram brushed thick hedges of fuchsia.

They took me young to learn a different language
far from those slopes red with bracken
where clearer water slides down levels of slate.

I remembered cairns where saints stood studying heaven,
dark galleries veined with gold and anthracite,
a saffron coastline littered with cowries and crab-shells,
those silhouetted castles, their high halls floored with grass.

Ships moor near a tower where lads play chess.
Shadows of heroes fight by the ruffled tarn.
A harper gives his message to the clouds.
I do not understand the words he sings.
I can no longer tell where I belong.

Not there where the legends have taken root,
not in my clanging birthplace, nor my adopted home,
not where I'm staying, nor where I want to be,
not where I travel to, nor the lands I've left,
not even there at last –
that green and windswept graveyard
where my forebears lie.

John Gurney

b. 1935, did National Service as a fighter pilot; Oxford-educated, and a teacher in both schools and Higher Education. The author of *Wheal Zion*, one of the most skilful and mature volumes of poems published by the well-respected Peterloo Poets; winner and runner-up in an armful of poetry competitions, both local and national; contributor to most of the important journals of our time; author of an epic unpublished poem *War* of 16,000 lines, more than twenty verse plays, and so many other poems as to be arguably even more prolific than Peter Redgrove, Jeremy Reed, or perhaps Peter Russell. A dozen years after *Wheal Zion* – a fine book largely ignored – Acumen Publications published his *An Average Revenge*, which seems to have lit something of a fresh fuse which, appropriately enough, burst into moderate flame with his next book *Coal* from Stride! He remains somewhat exiled by his art – the sheer monumentality of which is, perhaps, forbidding to even the biggest publishers and critics of our small age – but more attention is gradually being paid to his work. His principal gifts are great metrical facility; a rare capacity in our time to exactly match the spiritual idea with the concrete referent; and an ambition of scale that ranges easily between epic and sonnet. If his work has a weakness it is that his great energy is by no means always productive of 'eternal delight'. The head rather than the heart being most in evidence, there is sometimes a coldness about Gurney's work which makes him a poet more of alienation than celebration:

> I walk, disdaining sorrow, play my part;
> The classical detachment of the heart!

ECSTASY

Suddenly the sea's no more a place
for human dissolution. Limbs do not
evaporate, then vanish without trace
of life. The bay drains gracefully. The hot
sun's sunk. Time's immateriality
is changing mode. Oh, this is different –
this body, soft, elastic, beautifully
adapting to my thoughts, these feelings sent
like pulses through these terraces of glass
where William sits, translucent, finishing
an argument with darkness. Look! I pass
serenely through the fish-dock, following
the green wink of the buoy. I penetrate!
This dear interior life so permeates!

MISS ROSSETTI AT CHEYNE WALK

Things turned around when Miss Rossetti came.
Her moral melancholia calmed the zoo;
the peacocks ceased their screeching, guilt and shame
inhibited the active kangaroos
that frolicked in the garden. Swinburne's games
were quickly stopped, his limbs no longer flew
stark naked down the bannisters. Things tamed.
Grew seriously self-conscious and subdued.
The red-haired whore felt suddenly absurd;
the models felt uncovered, quickly dressed
like flesh trapped in a flash-house. Sadder than
old rain upon a grave, all hope deferred
her face was cold, aloof. Its eyes expressed
that there was nothing new beneath the sun.

THE SNIPE

This is where I'd come while you were being
analysed. I'd quietly stand
and stare down at the winter suffering
of the full Cam.
All seemed a reprimand,
too far from our monomial I AM.
As molecules of water shot the bridge,
perception seemed an act of sacrilege.

December, and the year had undergone
its final transformation.
The twigs were black as ink-sticks. Nothing shone.
The world seemed veiled
in bitter grey frustration.
Little was accomplished. Much had failed.
In water-meadows, hazed with frost and mist,
the willows seemed reluctant to exist.

I moved past Byron's pool toward the weir.
A crust of English ice
was bristling on its frozen barrier.
The dam seemed calm,
as still and deep as sleep,
as, mirror-still, with no sense of alarm,
it slid like time, then fell in ecstasy
through bends and yellow shallows, angrily.

A falling – that's what Heidegger once named
the gap between existence
and our essence – the fact that one is shamed
by what one is,
the nullity, the sense
of alienation from one's final bliss.
I'd failed you time again. You made me feel
all action was imperfect, ill, unreal.

And then, beside the black fault of a ditch,
I stumbled on the beauty
of a snipe. Its bright eyes dark as pitch,

it watched me down
its long, sad bill. Sacredly
it scanned the fissured shadows of my frown,
then bolted in a wild erratic flight
that flicked like schizophrenia, out of sight.

EFFIGIES

The all-in weight of Freud is forty pounds.
Life-size, made of wax and fibreglass,
he stoops here in the window through the sounds
of Conduit Street. Pedestrians, as they pass,
glance in at him. His figure's comforting.
Like Thought-for-Sale, in mustard-coloured tweeds,
an icon that's transcended suffering,
he spreads his wordless doctrine, speaks a creed
of Silence, as he studies, notes, observes:
is tranquil and alert, with perfect nerves.

Hypnotically his stillness draws me in.
My mind begins to question, starts to find
the dust upon his ears, his bearded chin.
The man who blew his eyes was colourblind –
the balls were hard to match. The sockets stared,
each Oedipal and empty, as they tried
to harmonise their shading. All his hair
is washable and soft, and neatly hides
the scar left by the surgeon. Half is yak's.
The shoes upon his feet are stained and black.

Resistance – yes. Old Rotto Rank was right.
We denigrate what we can't integrate,
prefer to work with magic. Frail and slight,
he stands there like the fixed idea of Fate,
a godhead we encounter when we try
to set ourselves in order, to deceive
the mad Id, and the Super-ego's cry
of strident accusation. He perceives

the nature of the process, how we're built.
His back bends with my own creative guilt.

Creative guilt. His sculptor sits apart.
She smokes there in a corner, cannot act:
has lost the will to make, to fashion art:
feels simple and diminished, inexact.
Undeified, and slowly humanised,
she feels the separation, powerless
to fabricate new forms. Uncanonised,
her hands, behind his back, are nonetheless
translucent. As they shine like inner air
they contradict the death-path of despair.

John Heath-Stubbs

b. 1918 in London. To be famous is not necessarily to receive the critical attention deserved for one's work. It is one of the great oddities and flaws of contemporary criticism that if a poet makes his or her name in a particular decade – as Heath-Stubbs did in the Forties – no matter how many books of poetry he or she may produce thereafter, they can be safely ignored. There are exceptions to this like Auden or Larkin (though even with them the decadist pigeon-holers worked overtime). As with James Kirkup, however, so with John Heath-Stubbs, in all the years I've known the latter and his work I've felt the critics have treated him rather like a distinguished portrait hung in a corner of the metropolitan House of Fame, occasionally to be glanced at, but mostly to be ignored. Leaving aside his considerable long poem *Artorius*, because long poems are always in some way controversial (c.f. E.A. Poe), Heath-Stubbs has produced an above-average number of highly accomplished and memorable short poems. It is true that he has received various honours for 'services to poetry' (whatever that may mean); but it is for his poetry alone that I include him; and to make the point that, all through the years of supposedly 'epoch-making' and 'definitive' anthologies designed to inform the public of the best contemporary poetry, his work has been too often omitted. Also because, despite being a recipient of the Queen's Gold Medal For Poetry, and being the current President of the Poetry Society of Great Britain, it is what a poet thinks and feels that finally matters; and in his 'Shepherd's Bush Eclogue' Heath-Stubbs speaks of '...each of us' as 'into continual exile travelling'. Sentiments which, I am sure, most, if not all, of the contributors to this anthology would echo.

IBYCUS

When the city cast out the best
    In a clamour of indecision,
I had no breath to waste
    Cobbling up their division;
I unhooked the lyre from its peg,
    Turned ship to the Samian shore.
I call no man to witness
    But the clanging birds of the air.

The quince-tree garden is shattered,
    The vine-shoots fail in Spring;
Down from the Thracian mountains,
    On fire with the lightning,
Love comes, like a blackguard wind.
    Love was betrayal and fear.
I call no man to witness
    But the clanging birds of the air.

The open-handed I praise,
    Great-souled Polycrates,
Pride of whose tinted galleons
    Ruled the Ionian seas.
Treachery took him – nailed
    For the crows to peck him bare.
I call no man to witness
    But the clanging birds of the air.

Twilight: a narrow place:
    Armed men blocking the road.
Gold glisters on my finger.
    In chevron high overhead
The southward-journeying cranes –
    What Erinnyes are here?
I call no man to witness
    But the clanging birds of the air.

A CHARM AGAINST TOOTHACHE

Venerable Mother Toothache
Climb down from the white battlements,
Stop twisting in your yellow fingers
The fourfold rope of nerves;
And tomorrow I will give you a tot of whisky
To hold in your cupped hands,
A garland of anise-flowers,
And three cloves like nails.

And tell the attendant gnomes
It is time to knock off now,
To shoulder their little pick-axes,
Their cold-chisels and drills.
And you may mount by a silver ladder
Into the sky, to grind
In the cracked polished mortar
Of the hollow moon.

By the lapse of warm waters,
And the poppies nodding like red coals,
The paths on the granite mountains,
And the plantation of my dreams.

SHEPHERD'S BUSH ECLOGUE

As I walked to Shepherd's Bush, I perceived it was truly pastoral,
For May, a Monna Vanna, a Mopsa, had tossed her cumuli,
Her flocks of white wool, into the azure and virginal
Fields of pure air that all over London lie.

I breathed a *Sursum Corda*; but a grief-worm in my breast
Twisted, and told me how all the riches of Spring
Are only a sandy fistful that runs through our fingers to waste;
For each of us is into continual exile travelling –

Moving away from life, and love, and lovers, and the light,

Since we fell from the primal garden into this troubled stream.
Not here, not here is our franchise: these images of delight
Still fail and fleet and cheat us in the context of a dream.

O Muse, I said then, dear sister, how long will your voice be mute?
This is your season, surely: these moments furnish your cue –
Praise this delicious weather with your accentor's throat;
In the heart of a poem's crystal alone can the Spring come true.

TO EDMUND BLUNDEN
on his 60th birthday

Thyrsis, or Meliboeus, or old Damoetas –
I must address you
By some such green, Virgilian-vowelled name –
You, the last and truly-tempered voice
Of all our lovely, dead, and pastoral England:
The radio brings that voice to me tonight,
Reading your poem, the vocables
With Kentish loam adhering to them still.
You on the Chinese shore, and I
In Alexandrian garboils? No –
For fourteen years are abrogated now;
The evening sun is gilding Abingdon,
And Kirk White's verse, and Bloomfield's, and Clare's
Our topic as we sit here in the bar,
And brown-haired boys are playing in the street.

1957

MOVING TO WINTER

As I move, through autumn to winter, my life's house
Is Edmund Waller's cottage of the soul.
How chill, how pure, eternity shines through the chinks!
Yet, while my fire still burns, I'll proffer

Scraps of toasted cheese to the crickets –
My long-legged, whiskery poems, that chirp in the crannies,
Or hop about on the flagstones. And there'll be other visitants –
    an incognito
Angel or so, all my accustomed ghosts.
And, twirling his forked tail, pedunculate-eyed,
With sharp, nine-inch proboscis for a nose,
Not all malignant, the odd domestic bogle.

UNICORN

With silver hooves and silken mane
    And spiral-twisted ivory horn,
Upon the crystal mountains, trots
    The solitary unicorn.

Nor gin nor snare can trip his heels,
    Nor is he any huntsman's game
Immaculately chaste, a virgin
    Alone can make that creature tame.

Beneath a sumptuous canopy
    A king of kings sat down to dine:
His most belov'd and trusted friend
    Stood by to fill his cup with wine –

His trusted friend? He should have known
    There's none that gold cannot suborn:
A deadly and slow-working poison
    Was slipped into his cup of horn.

Of unicorn horn that cup was fashioned,
    With cabbalistic signs engraved.
It splintered to a thousand pieces –
    But a royal life was saved –

And soon the traitors stood revealed,
    Who'd plotted to snuff out that life –

The trusted friend who bore his cup
    His son, his vizier, and his wife.

But on the far off crystal mountains,
    With blood-stained and dishonoured brow
Snared by a young girl's chastity
    The unicorn is weeping now.

THE DARK BIRDS

How I used to love those London crows –
Their raucous voices sounding
Over the mess of the post-war city.
I'd say "If there were truth in transmigration
I'd come back as a crow – there's nobody
That shoots them here, and plenty
Of rubbish for their dinners."

But now it is as if they were pre-figuring
This town's decline, a final agony
That could be worse than Babylon's or Rome's.

They seem like those black birds, flying on devil's wings
Out of the void, to scoff
The dried up seeds of faith and hope,
Among the dust that strews
The too-much trampled high-road of my life;
Or like that one that dogged the steps
Of Schubert's winter traveller, trudging
Into the frozen heart of things –
A hurdy-gurdy wheezing on the ice.

A.C. Jacobs

b. 1937 in Glasgow. He moved to London at the age of 14. He lived in Israel for three years in the early 60s, spent a considerable time in Scotland in the 70s, thereafter tending to divide his time between London and Madrid where, sadly, he died. Arthur Jacobs was an assiduous translator from the Hebrew poets, and from the Spanish; his translations of the Israeli poet David Vogel placing him among that relatively small band of translators in the twentieth century who have successfully managed to get across the poetic luminosity of original poetry from one language to another. His own poetry is quiet-toned and spare, and makes every word count to such a degree that – unlike more urgent and prolific poets who tend to prolixity, even slackness at times – the reader has the double pleasure of enjoying both word and sentiment in conscious parallel. As a Scots-Jew Arthur Jacobs' spiritual predicament could be compared to that of his fellow poet, the Welsh-Jew Dannie Abse, in the sharp and ever-deepening awareness – despite secularity – of the inherited cultural baggage of Judaism. For millenia it has been sufficient just to be a Jew to guarantee one's role as an exile, however much one may be assimilated or integrated into a particular society. And where one was, like Arthur Jacobs, also deeply versed in Scottish and English literature, self-identity became such a complex matter for both man and poet as to give additional force to the exile-outsider status.

OUT

All the poems not collected,
That are left lying in drawers
Among dying papers, or go roaming
On pages one can't recall,
Which of them really exist
And which are imagined?

When sortings take place they glow
And gnaw.

There should be some ceremony
Like *Kol Nidrei*, the solemn cancellation
Of all vows unaccomplished,
For these untended poems.

Whatever one owes them ought
To be erased.

PLEASE NOTE

I've never claimed great, accurate knowledge:
I've always lived in doubt,
But I haven't been quite as ignorant
As authorities have made out.

POEM FOR MY GRANDFATHER

On the Anniversary of His Death

Today, a candle in a glass
Burns slowly on the mantlepiece.
Wheesht, the dead are here.

My father, your grey-haired son,
Tastes again the salt, wax prayers
Of your sacred, dying day.

You are a name, holy in his presence,
The last solemn date
In our calendar of death.

Truly a ghost, my father sees, you.
A kind man's regret softens his face.

But for me there is no introduction:
For me you are a light on the mantlepiece,
A half shadow on the wall.

JERUSALEM

The town lies in its warm, blue evening,
I can feel the sleep of its easy stones.
There is a small white moon intoning
Put history by: call in your soul.

The dark, quiet streets, untense and shining,
Rock in their comfortable sounds.
The fury of martyred vision murmurs
Put grieving by: call in your soul.

The passion of these small, bare hills crying
On the last grief of Europe washed in them,
On fabulous, split energies shaping
Put searching by: call in your soul.

SOUND

In a rough, windy night
I have been listening
To the movements of the wind
And forming a kind of poem
Without knowing its language.

Ruach, I say, using
The old biblical word
For the wind, the breath
Or spirit of God
Moving after creation.

But nothing follows:
No other words
Cross the darkness outside.
There is only *ruach*,
The word for the sound of the wind.

NEW TOWN

In Heriot Row, on a misty November evening,
When the lamps were lit early in the cold damp
I passed the house of Stevenson and found
A metal plaque outside with a stanza of the poem
About Leerie I once knew.

I was glad
To remember that 'Child's Garden of Verses'
It came from, glad to remember the way
It was read to me, or I read it, long ago.

A most Stevensonian evening it was
As I walked along the pavement of that fine terrace

Back through my childhood in spaced out suburbs
That brought lives together and drove them apart.

James Kirkup

b. 1923 South Shields. For many years I read Kirkup's poetry knowing he was English, yet thinking of him as a latter-day Lafcadio Hern, a man who had passed beyond being a mere Japanophile and literally 'gone native': a view, I confess, formed in the late 60s by reading his volume *Paper Windows*. I remember talking about Kirkup with the late William Plomer, himself one of the first of the English poets to be invited to take up residence in Japanese university life; and Plomer confirmed this impression of just how 'native' Kirkup had become. When I read his recent Rockingham volume *Throwback* , which is subtitled 'Poems towards an Autobiography', I had a sense the very opposite of *deja vu*, for the poems are so thoroughly about his Tyneside origins, despite the poet's almost total disappearance out of his own culture. Actually, a friend and I wondered jocularly if 'James Kirkup' really existed, or if it was a situation like Pessoa with his many heteronyms: a spectacularly successful instance of a pseudonym being operated by some other poet. We thought of Kirkup's lines 'Few people have ever met me / fewer still know my name' – only the first part true though! Levity apart, however, operating so closely between two cultures but apparently writing in one, having translated innumerable works from many languages, over-publishing his own poetry because of that facility he has (so beautifully understated by James Dickey when he said: 'With Kirkup's work I don't feel that facility is the problem'), and that sense of urgency to 'get it all down' which comes to the much-travelled writer, are a reflection of this unique exile's 'crisis of identity' which has led to the question as to who or what is James Kirkup? Maybe, too, it accounts for the aenemic sense (of having spread himself too thinly) I get about a lot of his work – even as early as *The Drowned Sailor* or *The Submerged Village*, both works mainly of the 1940s; and for why, later, he was so strongly attracted to that most refined of concrete expressionism, the *haiku*? Maybe it *also* accounts for the exquisitely melancholic rhythm that suddenly surfaces in *Throwback*, and gives us some of his best work? At any rate, I doubt anyone is better qualified for inclusion in this anthology than Kirkup: the perfect exile of the jet-setting age.

TRANSATLANTIC FLIGHT

The hostess, with sickening self-possession,
Puts us unwillingly at ease, as if
It was nothing, all this noise and trundling
Over cement that turns before we know it
Into the bumpy road of air.

The city lurches under us, the map tilts,
Demonstrates a broader scale, and yet
Contracts, as we do. The river
Swivels in a bomb-flash sun, and seems
To rear against the paralysed sea.

The trustful passengers obediently relax,
Turn back their watches gaily to the time
Of the country they are bound for, inviting
Fate. – But one, whose every breath becomes
His last, a heavy sigh,

Thinks only of the earth, the lost night
Where he must wake and die.

WREATH MAKERS: LEEDS MARKET

A cocksure boy in the gloom of the gilded market bends
With blunt fingers a bow of death, and the flowers work with him.
They fashion a grave of grass with dead bracken and fine ferns.

An old woman with a mouthful of wires and a clutch of irises
Mourns in perpetual black, and her fists with the sunken rings
Rummage in the fragrant workbasket of a wreath.

A laughing Flora dangles a cross between her thighs
Like a heavy child, feeds it with pale plump lilies, crimson
Roses, wraps it in greenery and whips it with wires.

And here a grieving flower god with a lyre in his arms

Fumbles mute strings in the rough-gentle machine of his fingers,
His eyes wet violets, and in his mouth a last carnation…

Mourners all, they know not why they mourn,
But work, and breathe the perfumes of their trade
(Those flower-voices, through which death more keenly speaks)

With suitable dispassion; though they know their emblems fade,
And they at last must bear a yellowed wreath
That other hands, and other harvesters have made.

SWAN LEGENDS

The swan sings at his lonely death among
The islands of an archipelago
Or in a northern forest lit with snow
Speaks of the darkness in his final song.

Or when his fellow swan has died, (their long
Silences broken), rising on slow,
Strong wings, he soars into the afterglow
Of that deep summer where all deaths belong.

Higher he climbs, till he can fear no more
The dark that bears him, with his love, away;
He flies into the stars, and sings alone,
Then folds the wings that will no longer soar,
And with one last wild cry, through endless day
Thunders down miles of darkness, like a stone.

THE SAND ARTIST

On the damp seashore
above the rainbows of shells, seaweed, seacoal,
the sandman wanders, seeking for a pitch.

Ebb-tide is his time. The sands are lonely,
but a few lost families
camp for the day on its Easter emptiness.

He seeks the firm sand of the retreating wave.
They, with their sandwiches and flasks of tea,
lay their towels upon the dry slopes of dunes.

From the sea's edge he draws a pail
of bitter brine, and carries it carefully
towards the place of first creation.

There he begins his labours. Silent,
not looking up at passing shadows
or curious children, he moulds his dreams.

No simple sandcastles melting as they dry,
but galleons, anchors, liners, cornucopias,
mermaids, Neptunes, dragons of the deep.

With a piece of stick, a playing card
and the blunt fingers of a working man
the artist draws existence into being from the sea.

As the returning tide takes back his gifts,
he waits in silence by his pitman's cap
for pennies from the sky.

Ocean Road sands

VARIATIONS ON A THEME BY ROBERT DESNOS

Today I went walking with a friend.
We walked by the river, under the trees,
along the beach and over the rocks
to the end of the pier with its crashing seas –
along the quaysides and the silent docks.

Today I went walking with a friend.
I showed him secret places I had always known
and told him tales that I had never told.
Our words and laughter on the wind were blown
until the night fell and the town was cold.

Today I went walking with a friend.
It was the first time we had walked together –
and the last. For I never saw his face again,
or heard his voice. And now, in lonely weather,
I walk alone, my only friend the rain, the rain.

– But once I went walking with a friend.

FROM HEROIC FURIES

Love gives me
such visions of
cold truth
it opens for me
sombre doors
of wisdom beyond
thought or
feeling when
the divinity
enters me
to be reborn
to grow
slowly into
poetry within
his endless reign

Lotte Kramer

b. 1923 Maine, Germany; she became a Jewish refugee from Nazi Germany who ended up taking British citizenship. Before the founding of the State of Israel after World War 2, all Jews had exile as their birthright – their 'song' was rootless long before the modern world was thought of. Those Jews who, like Lotte Kramer and many millions more, were driven from their continental homelands by the Nazi persecution in our time, are doubly exiles. Lotte Kramer has expressed this with devastating simplicity in her poem 'Aspects Of Home':

> But mostly home
> Is where we meet:
> In unseen countryside
> From chance to word.

Unlike many poet-refugees from the Holocaust, Lotte Kramer has developed in her poetry an appreciative tenderness for the natural landscape of her place of exile. Indeed, were it not for the fact that her work continues to be haunted, from time to time, by both her land of birth, Germany, and the Holocaust, one would have little difficulty placing her work firmly in that Wordsworthian tradition of English poetry. I have always thought Lotte Kramer a good poet, but one of too modest pretensions; not because she so well marries the suffering of the dispossessed Jew with that calmer strain of English nature poetry, but because – like so many contemporary poets bred much nearer to home – she appears to think of English poetry as, essentially, a passionless and modest affair whose true representatives are Edward Thomas and Philip Larkin, rather than Shakespeare and Milton. In another age, and one with a less reductive and restrictive view prevailing, the gifted emigrant and exile, such as Lotte Kramer, would have developed more forcefully and considerably.

ON READING SOME NEWS BEFORE A TRAIN JOURNEY

(Jan Palach's body was removed secretly)

Somewhere they moved a body overnight.
Somewhere they robbed a grave in secrecy
Because they fear his gutted flesh, his light.

I see a golf-course flashing by outside
And men launching a ball, deliberately;
Somewhere they moved a body overnight.

Across the table, manicured and tight,
Hands hold 'The Times' in anonymity
Because they fear his gutted flesh, his light.

Along a corridor a black boy slides
In search for something else – maybe some tea;
Somewhere they moved a body overnight.

A busty girl in red, her man and child
Sit on my left quite wordlessly
Because they fear his gutted flesh, his light.

The landscape that escapes is fixed outside;
In here the breath of each passivity:
Somewhere they moved a body overnight
Because they fear his gutted flesh, his light.

ASPECTS OF HOME

Home is in this field,
This quietness
That confiscates all else.
Here shadows mark
Solidity –
Machinery content
To know its route –
As though our feet

Could tread this earth for ever.
To lose this clay
Would blind me, lock
The sky into the night.
But mostly home
Is where we meet:
In unseen countryside
From chance to word –
And filter thoughts
We never hoped to enter.

WOMEN IN DRESS SHOPS

They come in eager to confide.
Baring their bodies,
Part of their confession,
Each sagging limb a pediment.

And from their outer wools and tweeds
That camouflage the scent
Hiding detection
Down to the intimates of flesh

They spend themselves; because at last
They're able to obtain
An ear, an interest
That will flatter them expensively.

Later, when they have left the shop,
Each tale still travels on
In darts, and hems, and pleats,
To its own hushed senility

While we, with empty echoes, take
The threads and wrap them round
Our own fragilities
To toughen up the seams of love.

THE LAST OF WINTER

Today, the last of winter,
Your letter came, telling me
How you seek the sun outside
Your house now, no longer able
To travel South, so you sit on a chair
In the street for two hours, watching,
Absorbing the yellow goodness,
And gratitude breaks from your lines.

You tell me, too, of another
Who died in his sleep having
Completed his four score and five
In a museum of simplicity,
Who has travelled through many
Languages and was able to age
With his own house and land,
And his wife's quiet tears.

So I went out to the black earth
Beaded with gulls and snow,
To the high river returning
The sky's reel, inhaling
A slow sharpening of air
Where the profile of death had been seared,
Grateful for each footstep from
The streets of winter, for a face.

COCOON

She says she can't remember anything
Of people, language, town. Not even school
Where we were classmates. Her smile is frail
And hides behind her husband's hypnotising

Quietness. 'A Suffolk man', he beams
And squares his tweedy frame against some

Unseen advocates who might still claim
An inch of her. She is content, it seems,

To lose her early childhood; he is near.
Protector or destroyer, it's his war.
He underwrites her willed amnesia,
Helps to stifle terror, exile, fear.

She is cocooned, safe as an English wife
Never to split that shell and crawl through love.

BILINGUAL

When you speak German
The Rhineland opens its watery gates,
Lets in strong currents of thought.
Sentences sit on shores teeming
With certainties. You cross bridges
To travel many lifetimes
Of a captive's continent.

When you speak English
The hesitant earth softens your vowels.
The sea – never far away – explores
Your words with liquid memory.
You are an apprentice again and skill
Is belief you can't quite master
In your adoptive island.

Myself, I'm unsure
In both languages. One, with mothering
Genes, at once close and foreign
After much unuse. Near in poetry.
The other, a constant love affair
Still unfulfilled, a warm
Shoulder to touch.

Dinah Livingstone

b. North Devon, but came to London in 1966, and has been a familiar figure around the literary metropolis ever since then. She founded the Camden Voices poetry group, and has been most closely associated with that area of London just to the north of St. Pancras Station for a long while now. The *persona* which emerges from her poetry is that of a country girl who has become thoroughly urbanised. Dinah Livingstone is not so much an exile – except in the general sense that all poets, because of the solitary nature of their calling, are exiles – as one who has suffered critical neglect for a very definite, but important reason which I wish to highlight because it makes her something of a representative figure for our time. The principal weakness occasionally marring her poetry is that ease, even slackness, of verbal arrangement characteristic of what is known as 'performance poetry'. Where immediacy of communication is the over-riding impulse behind a poem, rather than the absolute necessity generated by what Laura Riding called 'the poem-event', then the arrangement of the words will be over-simplified in meaning and in clarity of verbal effect. (One encounters a similar flattening of rhythm and effect in poets who devote too much time to translation work.) The primary motive of, and impulse for, a poem, in order for it to become a genuine and durable artefact, has to be truth-and-feeling; and pleasure, delight, entertainment, statement, etc., are subordinate to that essential seriousness of intent: they are but the by-products of a primary compound, as chemists might say. Performance poetry subordinates the free ranging poetic inspiration to some secondary purpose – like 'message' or 'entertainment' – and elevates such latter to primacy of place. The result is a slackening of the essential poetic pattern (and rhythm) which, as long as the poet is present to recite the work aloud, can often be overcome. Naked on the page, however, without props of any kind, this weakness is soon apparent. In Dinah Livingstone's case her poems not infrequently suffer in this way, but I have endeavoured to choose poems which have a 'page-life' of their own – which all true poems should have.

TO MY CAMDEN POETRY GROUP

Yes, I am nasty, I admit you're right,
I get bad tempered at poor quality,
I hurt when I'm impatient for delight,
please take account of human frailty.
But now that powers of darkness threaten doom,
let me salute each individual voice
stuttering for utterance in this tatty room:
we are the living, come let us rejoice.
For if this Christmas here a child is born
in bare simplicity, its name is Hope,
who will have many mothers, not just one
madonna, fathers too, since god can't cope.
We are, we make the word and hence may love;
there is no other trinity above.

WOMAN IN A DRESSING GOWN

On the keen edge of morning
she does not dance,
no angel, more of a mist drifting.
In what sense does she exist?
A noise of passions ringing her for dead:
she can't get dressed.

She takes tea back to bed,
covets more rest.
Unshod, ungirded, unsafe fuzzy head,
she senses both at once
why Antony disarmed for dying,
Cleopatra dressed.

ROWAN TREE

Three boulders of granite
step over the stream
where the steep path hairpins
at the head of the combe.

Islanded here, splendid
in all its full-berried vermilion,
filtering sun through eager green,
glowed the rowan tree,
magic and exigent
as when for True Thomas
it marked the choice of ways.

I kept still, filled my eyes,
listened to water
and for red deer,
waited to be told. What?

When the bright ordeal burnt out
I munched cold bun and cheese.
Later in London another rowan
shone among drab donkey brown
of terraces and pavement slabs
recently rinsed by rain.
Clearer with second sight.

ST PANCRAS LOCK

A delicious boy fishing
perched on the slippery lock wall edge,
sound of rushing water under him,
roses and English marigolds
in the keeper's cottage garden,
dilapidated barges
some got up with tat.

Across the canal adolescent
willows reserve the wildlife
where Ken introduced newts
and to my left the giant gasometers
with their iron tracery painted red.
I sit on a towpath bench,
nod to odd cyclists sizzling to Islington.

Like everyone here
I have come on my own
wishing some things, faintly melancholy
at this shabby tranquil Victorian corner
where greenery grows dusty with summer
and the dim hum I am content to be part of
is the spirit of London.

MAY DAY

A May morning at Minsmere,
in the bird reserve, many calls
I can't identify – some singing,
some sound more conversational
and the bass is the rhythm of the sea.

Before me in young leaf the May tree
stands frothing with starry blossom
milky sunlit epiphany:
in admiration hope does not fail.

The tree is thick and squat,
its comfortable shape
tousled on top
spikes the hazy blue
now clearing to speedwell.

Its flowering mouth
opens with that annual outburst
of belief in life before death,

faith leading to insight
of a species as whole-heartedly human
as it is most tranquilly tree.

Of course they want to cancel it.
These bosses despise
workers, makers, seers,
deny their holiday.
Time runs out on earth.
May Day. May Day. May Day…

Edward Lowbury

b. London 1913; took degrees in physiology and medicine at Oxford, where he also won the Newdigate Prize for poetry. There is a sense in which practising a major profession – other than poetry itself – can, for a poet, increase the sense of being an exile both in the literary world and in life. This is especially true of medicine which is arguably the most inherently vocational of conventional professions. (Indeed I can recall , when I was younger, the way that doctors and nurses – especially matrons – would use the term 'laymen' to emphasise their sense of apartness from the world of their patients.) However, in order to achieve anything in art an almost overwhelming commitment is required, so the doctor-poet has to endure a condition – which may be lifelong – of something like a divided psyche. Among the poets of our time who are also medical men, Dannie Abse and Edward Lowbury are the outstanding names in Britain. It is my belief that both have been accorded a degree of recognition for their work as poets while, at the same time, their work as physicians has led to their typecasting as 'doctor-poets', in a way analogous to what can happen to actors through being too closely associated with a single role on television. Nobody bothered much that Larkin was a librarian, Eliot a bank clerk, or Auden a teacher, but – somehow – being a doctor intrudes on the poetry. Lowbury has been publishing volumes of verse since the 1930s from large and small presses; poetry of skill and quality; yet his work has been mostly absent from the fashionable anthologies of the intervening decades; nor has it received the critical attention one might have expected for one so active in literature. His inclusion here, among our band of exiles and independents, helps to round the picture of what's been happening a little more, and may gain him better recognition for the fine prosodist he is; and also because he is one of that select number of poets who has improved with age: *especially* since his retirement from medicine.

THE NIGHT WATCHMAN

That old man – I must have seen him somewhere:
  A battered scarecrow, but he draws my glance
    From things worth looking at,
And nods to me with a faintly mocking air.

And now I seem to remember the lost link:
  It's Nick, the night watchman:
    At five I pestered him 'How old are you?'
And he answered, grinning, 'Older than you think.'

My guess was – 'a hundred.' Our next meeting
  Was after twenty years;
    He seemed no older then – perhaps less old:
I caught his eye, but he passed without a greeting.

Twenty years on, and here he comes again,
  Almost unchanged; at first I try to avoid
    His glance, but can't resist;
Then catch his eye with a quick jab of pain:

It's a shock to find that now I don't seem
  So far behind old Nick in years;
    He nods to me this time... When next we meet
I think I shall have overtaken him.

SPRING-CLEANING AT SEVENTY

I'm burning up the past, this load of letters;
  Stop now and then to read a page or two.
A few I'll save. What meant so much, those matters
  Of moment, like 'we are pleased to offer you
The post...' – they bore me now; even messages
  Of friendship read like slogans, hollow stuff;
Nor am I shattered by such passages
  As 'Yes, I like you, but that's not enough'.

A crumpled yellow sheet drops from the pile,
  An unfamiliar hand. I smooth it out
And try to read the faded script: '...your smile
  Haunts me... when you are with me I could shout
For joy... you say "be happy", but I can't –
  You are always in my thoughts, but you're not here';
Signed 'Mary Keats', the writing diffident,
  Shaky, ink-blurred – maybe a tear.

Then suddenly I race back forty years
  To a night ward-round in my hospital
Where Sister Keats has briefed me; next, my ears
  Pick up the distant song of a nightingale
Through the open window, and a crazy whim
  Prompts me to read John Keats to Mary Keats, –
I feel that I'm reciting it to him! –
  While far away that nightingale competes.

But Mary Keats is savouring every line,
  Mirrors in those dark eyes each syllable,
Letting them rest luxuriously on mine.
  'I did not know it was so rich, so full',
She whispers...
                    That was forty years ago:
  Then I believed it was the Ode which gave
Such colour to her cheeks, but I was slow;
  My cheeks burn now. – Her letter I will save.

IN THE TRAIN

In a train to Dover the old man sits facing
A girl; admires her looks but turns away
    From a shape that still can spark desire –
A useless function now... There was a day
When such a glance could lead to something good:
    He reaches back, recalls a chance
Encounter, in a Paul Jones, with the eyes
Of an unknown beauty at a college dance.

But now he notices this girl's reflection
In the carriage window, a pale transparency,
A disembodied wraith, proper
Companion for the ghost he has come to be; –
Looks hard at the lovely apparition
Without guilt or embarrassment,
Stares with a joyful newborn innocence
At – and right through her to the fields of Kent.

SPECTRE OF A ROSE

Nature abhors a vacuum, fills the islands
Of blindness in this eye
With pictures, as she fills with sounds
Others can't hear a deaf man's actual silence.

Sometimes I half-see, above my field
Of vision, a china plate,
Worcester or Delft; it vanishes
If I try to see it but if, instead, I shield

My eyes or gaze ahead, the phantom fades
Gradually; later
It's there again, above the page
I'm reading, blue-and-white, or subtler shades.

Today a terrier is what I half-see –
Frisking along the pavement
Ahead of my right foot; I know
It isn't there, but automatically

Mutter 'I'm sorry' when my shoe comes close
To kicking the apparition...
Then a gentler phantom takes
The terrier's place – the spectre of a rose.

AN OLD PHOTOGRAPH

For James Hogg

Fifty years old, that photo picturing me
  At ease on the carpeted deck of a Persian dhow
    In old Mombasa harbour, the Captain's guest:

We drink black coffee; hallowed rules allow
  Three cups, no less, – no more even if you're pressed!
    Oddly, that ancient photo looks more real

Than the present hour. That island of the blest,
  Mombasa remembered, an image of the ideal,
    Is a snatch of eternity, and the youthful face

In the picture, so much sprightlier than I feel
  Today, must have materialised to replace
    My ageing image with a bolder print.

Its mark is permanence, without a trace
  Of change through fifty years, without a hint
    Of wear-and-tear. Unlike the countenance

I own, this is a coin fresh from the mint,
  Its print still sharp: its mark is permanence;
    And I could half-believe the real 'I'

Is that still picture, not this transience,
  The real 'now' that spell of dark blue sky
    In old Mombasa harbour, where I sip

Black coffee, sit in warm tranquility
  On Persian carpets on that Persian ship,
    Talking with the Master through interpreters, –

    That is, until Time gives us all the slip.

Alexis Lykiard

b. Athens 1940; came to England at the age of 6, and won a scholarship to King's College, Cambridge at 17 where he edited *Granta* magazine. In 30 years he has produced more than a dozen volumes of poetry, but has – critically speaking – paid the price of being better known as a novelist and translator than as a poet. *Summer Ghosts*, his most famous fiction work, made him something of a cult figure on the Sixties' scene, and like Adrian Mitchell, Michael Horovitz, and a number of other figures from those years, Lykiard has been typecast by time. In terms of poetry the Sixties' principal allegiance was to the Beats, and insofar as Alexis Lykiard has continued loyal to the likes of Jack Kerouac, Lawrence Ferlinghetti, and William Burroughs, so he has voluntarily contributed to that radical typecasting. Nevertheless, his poems have appeared in many quarters not at all sympathetic to the Beats or Sixties' counter-culture; and such is implicit recognition that his poetry often possesses less ephemeral and more traditional qualities such as timelessness, sharp wit, and deft metrical skills. Something which – but for critical neglect – would have been more fully recognised before:

> Now when strange speech surrounds us, sounds
> we can't understand, words to unnerve us, alien all,
> no wonder we seek formless benediction often:
> the whispered prayer for peace through every cypress,
> the calming surf outside our shack's thin door,
> an ancient cat's affectionate low purr.
> Faced with the gutteral world's weird usage
> we must make choices, crack or soften,
> longing for our own tongues to meet, for
> our sweet precious private language, once again,
> for love, whose touch will tell us who we are.

Well known, too, as a translator from the French, the uncommon range of his own poetry, with its distinct voice, is becoming more fully appreciated.

SECOND THOUGHTS

> In June, amid the golden fields,
> I saw a groundhog lying dead.
> *Richard Eberhart*

A glossy American calendar adorns the kitchen wall,
colour plates to leaf through, assorted Impressionists.
At first I cannot for the life of me see why the 2nd
February in clear if modest lettering insists,
lest we forget, that it's come round again, has Groundhog Day.

I never would have imagined, let alone reckoned,
a day was anywhere devoted to the marmot, mousy animal.
The word groundhog (I'd thought) meant hedgehog, after all,
though perhaps of a larger kind, found mainly in the USA.
How wrong I was in my long misreading! So today,

due date noted – while over *there* it may well be Groundhog Day,
still I'll praise our erinaceous natives, those nocturnalists;
watch out for them dusk and dawn, in prickly summers when they root
for larvae and snails, slugs, worms or fallen fruit.
Flea-ridden, fearful they reshape, ball into spiked fists:

pointless the roadhog flattening them, when for a start
our absurd urchins do no harm in their, at most, six-year span.
Besides, the lowly hedgepig (as christened in this part
of Devon) has enemies enough, badger and fox – not counting man.
I continue to cherish the earthen-coloured, pointy creature

for another more personal and far obscurer reason.
Years back, shy, set on edge, we were made to learn by rote
that then inscrutable anthology piece by Richard Eberhart.
My startled, hibernating schoolboy wits shuffled with such a slow
pace toward the thorny gist of his fine, unexpected poem

that I could just about sense strange new-worldly pain, go
like its rarely-glimpsed subject, dumbly alert,
myopic to locate the space which finally was home.
Ever since, words have crawled into shape so – I can
shift or place them in the way of a certain hedgehog for whom

my son and myself once left milk at the end of the garden.
"Do your utmost," folk might have affirmed, "to cause these no harm."
Words weren't needed. Something unsaid replaces school or teacher,
and with a smiling boy's arm linked in my own right arm,
I returned to the warm house. Tonight, marking the chill season,

mindless fear might lurk, apt always to clutch at any throat,
leaching bright colour, leaving a speechless husk to assert
that lone small things live under threat. In this great pursuit
darkness is sure to descend, frost must duly harden
upon absence, a dish licked clean, and what remains of
Groundhog Day.

THE ART OF CAPTAINCY

Retiring in both senses, the old groundsman spoke:
– I still recall my first big game
of cricket for the County team.
I was our youngest wouldbe pro
though all of us went in some awe
of Walter Hammond, skipper then.
(General you might say, to enlisted men!)
Sent out to field, it proved no joke,
the batsmen hammered us and I let through
several hard shots which flew for four.
That endless afternoon nothing was good,
Gloucester turned Hell under the sun.
I froze, some sweated, others swore.
Blushing in the Pavilion, I tried to apologize.
"Really I'm sorry, Mr Hammond sir, I should
have kept my legs together." "No,
lad", the Great Man answered, slow
and loud, his timing sweet, fire in his eyes:
"That's what your mother should have done."

ADVICE TO A NEW WRITER

Stay proud, never reveal a tender heart.
Patiently play the cynic from the start,

and thus when disappointment is your due
no fool can laugh or lord it over you.

Take pleasure in your work: you won't be rich,
since publishers are crooks and fame a bitch.

Beware, if young and handsome, for good looks
only ensure that most men hate your books;

worse still, you'll lose that precious inch of space
should jealous rivals once recall your face,

while critics – barren cuckolds – aim reviews
against a husband faithful to the Muse.

Ignored, abused, or broke, you will discover
the book world loves a eunuch, not a lover.

A FUTURE FOR ALEXANDER

Up in my study, sun distracts. I stare,
stop tapping noisy keys, leave the machine
and let that dialogue dangle in mid-air:
I need to fix what else I may have seen.

My clumsy dancer does a cossack crouch,
rises to stagger up the steep-banked lawn.
A plastic plant-pot's the red prize for each
small fist to clutch. When he was born

those tight-furled fingers blossomed, swift to touch
my cheeks as if to drink the moisture there.

Two years ago... Love's deepening roots are such
that we both learn: delight is knowing where

to look. Battling the slope, he stumbles, spills
a boisterous peace-cry, grips his grenades
of harmless pleasure, challenging the hills
and charging the green gradient. Bliss fades

too fast, like the impatient rush to be
whatever hero he imagines he
is meeting, fighting or becoming and
whose helmet he now bears in either hand.

Reality is myth. I'll tell the boy –
observed through irises so mauve-and-blue,
signs of bruised beauty framed as shapes of joy
alive, ungathered in the garden – "You

don't need words like Purpose yet. Everything
spears into imperial purple, life's good
war. You thrust at, cleave the clear hill air, bring
splendid resourcefulness to Might or Could.

Over the valley, cloud shadows do move
but nothing cools your ardour. Laugh or cry
with sheer loud zest, you've so much new to prove,
birds sing, and nothing threatens from that sky..."

Just then a jet roars by – and words end here.
I go downstairs for lunch: concern and fear
churn in my gut and concentrate my brain.
When must sons learn and by what means, that pain

is inescapable on earth? I know
though, kneeling, head bowed to receive his kiss,
how precious life is: I was born for this,
simply to share him, love him, watch him grow.

DISTRACTIONS

Has my ex-wife mad cow disease?
    She wants to give me hell
and reckons having money frees
    her from restraint as well.

I get threats through solicitors
    to brighten up the day.
Writing me letters without pause
    they will not go away,

since she pays them to harass me,
    distract me from my work.
Hired jokers can't embarrass me:
    that thought drives her berserk.

Resentment makes one play dull games;
    she has not much to do
and idleness simply inflames
    a limited world view.

Might some new suitor interest
    her? Fat chance! Truth to tell,
they keep wise distance, while my best
    revenge is living well.

Richard O'Connell

b. 1928 in New York City; served in the U.S. Navy during the Korean War, and later attended Writing Seminars at Johns Hopkins University. He taught English for 18 years at Temple University, Philadelphia, where he also edited *Poetry Newsletter*: an international periodical of translations and original poetry. Probably the only academic in modern times to have lost his university post for lampooning his superiors in epigrams, and getting them published in *Playboy* magazine. His verse has appeared in many periodicals, and is characterised throughout by vigorous powers of expression, a good ear for rhythm, and a propensity to experiment in modes as different as the narrative poem, the monologue, and the hard-edged imagist fragment. For me, O'Connell is at his best in solid lyric poems which have a strong musical punch, and in his epigrams, which often have real bite. *Retro Worlds*, his recently published selected poems (University of Salzburg), is a quite outstanding and individual volume. I can only conclude the critical neglect accorded this poet's work is due to that prevailing climate (about which Dana Gioia has written so compellingly) in America which is too inhospitable to work possessed of strong formal properties, and to the fact of O'Connell's fiercely independent spirit manifested in his satirical epigrams.

ANNUNCIATION

Nobody blamed her. When a god comes down
What can a poor girl do? For who can block
His will? She never had a chance to think
Knocked senseless by that enervating shock
Of lightning, she woke crying on the ground;
And then it was so simple and so clear:
She felt a blossom crushing underneath
Her body, warm blood running, and no fear.

A golden swarm of suns swam in his eyes
And all the sky was covered by his head;
And she, delirious. Well, you know the rest.
The cataclysm left her nearly dead.
Then nothing! only desert, bitter sand…
Her belly buckled. She still felt his weight.
But where was he? She looked up at the sky.
He left her as a god does: full of fate.

NORTH

Nobody sleeps. Up here in summer time
the naked sunlight hammers on your skull
so fierce you can't stay out in it for long –
till like the town you end up slumped in dark
and smoke at the gigantic Gateway Bar.
Brash kids crowd in, all headed for the mines,
red-faced as infants – hungry innocents.
Old roustabouts sit silent in their chairs:
they're iced-in still – wedded to night and cold
and murder undetected. Which hasn't killed
with gun or knife or maybe with bare hands?
The frozen lakes lock secrets in their skulls.

While Eskimos chaw beer like so much blubber
at the back tables – grinning Genghis Khans –
ferocious in their furs and moon-pocked faces,

a waitress shivers like a tropic fish
among barbed glances – chilled down to her marrow.
I swallow my sixth or seventh glass of beer
watching the Go-Go girl from Winnipeg
baring her boyish torso to the bold
applause of fists and stomping feet. Go! Go!
Only the waiters, slinging trays of foam
in rolled shirt-sleeves, seem in touch with the real
and most of all the owner "Baby Face"
perched high, impassive as a totem god.

Wearily I climb to bed, not even drunk,
collapsing in bright daylight. Wide awake
I sob an endless dream of loss and death.

THE APOTHEOSIS OF DON JUNE

Promiscuous as moonlight on the sand
He pondered heaven by the foaming surf;
And staring at its brilliant text he saw
He'd never been voluptuous enough.

There were so many things his soul had missed
By never standing still and tasting life
– By frantically accepting the flat role,
Forgetting he was maker of his myth.

The night was warm, he breathed each fragrant smell.
What if no señorita stroked his wrist
And flattered the steel of his greying hair
– He knew how more than ever he flashed male.

How unimportant his small conquests, lusts
– Was not this placid life the sweetest tryst?
He puffed his cigarillo – live red sparks
Flew up as his charred ashes sought the stars.

STOPOVER IN BELÉM

It's hard to believe the Amazon is home
For that bent figure fishing from a rock
Before you hit the runway in Belém;

For him the Amazon's a mess of flesh
And little else but a benevolent brown breast
To suck at – throbbing, lethally alive;

Ignoring the rich thunder of your engines
And maybe dozing under his straw hat
Dreaming of some enormous dazzling queen.

A cold beer in the airport of Belém
Is one way to inhabit earth again
And merge your hunger with the fisherman's.

Still it's hard to believe those palms are real
Shivering across the almost molten lake
Of asphalt where your jet sits swilling fuel –

As sitting in the steam bath of Belém
You feel the gross weight of the physical
Noting the essential sameness of each scene.

And hard and harder still to accept each take-off
– The fierce detachment of the torrid sun
Wheels up and wheeling the wide Amazon:

The routine thunder over humdrum jungle –
The blazing depths of your incredible Brazil
And the eternal tyranny of green.

U.S. OASIS

Suddenly unarmed of their cars
they stand in a stupor
gorging hotdogs and cokes;
faces astringent, afraid –
all trying somehow to remain
untouched by each other.

Quickly relieved they step
outside; dazed, blinded by heat –
suffocating in a vast vacant landscape
where the turnpike
roaring twists toward the next mirage.

Brian Louis Pearce

b. Acton, London 1933; educated at Acton County School and University College. Spent his effective working life as a librarian. Acton, Kew, Richmond, and Twickenham remain the nub of his world. A man of the Thames in her most beautiful moods, Pearce is also a committed christian. He is the author of *Victoria Hammersmith,* a masterpiece among experimental novels; 'Coombe Hill', a beautifully crafted poem that is also a philosophical meditation; and many books of poetry, both traditional and experimental. In him the true flame burns: but encased in a genuine humility, even a shyness; which has placed him at the furthest possible remove from what Robert Graves called 'the career poet'. This has resulted in his considerable achievement going largely unrecognised in a world where critics seem bent on following the wrong signs. As Pearce says in his poem 'Thames Music': 'Few, indeed, have loved the light'; though he has, hence his neglect. In Pearce's case I suspect a quiet desperation at being ignored has led to the compensatory self-justification of publishing too much. Which is to say, much that should have found its way to the waste basket, not to the book: a sure sign of lack of self-criticism – artistically speaking. Yet there is a strong vein of fine ore discoverable throughout his work, but nowhere more than in the exquisitively balanced lines of the aforementioned 'Coombe Hill':

> Slowly, I climb; slowly, the hill
> Of ancient, monumental Coombe
> Sinks down beneath my feet
> And drifts beneath my gaze, until,
> Heart level with the sky, there's room
> For God and man to meet.

Such fine pointing of each delicate cadence runs through all of that poem, and is the especial talent of Pearce's, carried endlessly on into ever more adventurous and experimental pieces. For such an especial proclivity alone would he be worth reading – though there is much more to this dedicated craftsman than that.

THAMES LISTENER

There is no music
either at Boulter's Lock
at Greenwich, or past Gravesend

There is no sound
except that music heard
by one who listens for it

by one who listens for it all his life

banks of green willow
white walls
the wide and widening reaches
and dark swell
passing Reculver's towers

There is no music
except for one man, listening all his life
from the first ripple to the Sirens' swell
to the sense of the faint stir
in order that he might, however failingly,
attempt to re-create it. All this music,
from its sources to the estuary,
is given us through him. Without him,
the dreamer or musician, Syrinx, poet,
there is no music.
It is only heard
by those who listen and believe in it.

It is in the listener's spirit
It is here, in the pit of being
under the heart
It is the music
heard aforetime
but never quite recalled
down here in the city
music such as a man
may (O so yearningly) grasp at
only

to miss (at times, O so narrowly)

passing Reculver's towers

There is no music

but there is.

RUNAWAYS

Cars screech. Two horses have broken
loose to graze in the lane.
Can a woman's soft speech, or a token
of stick, secure them again?

Runaway horses, let loose
in the chalk and flint of the track.
Blue horses of Marc? I choose
his timidest deer, that looks back,

rather than these archetypes
of a future we bring on ourselves,
that daily draws nearer, that rips
all that our culture involves.

Bridles in shreds, they're away,
tossing our faith like a load
of wet straw. We're at bay,
and the future is chewed in the road.

TO VÈRA OUMANÇOFF

To me, it is always the last day;
that's why I never look forward,
or see it all quite like the others:
that's why I'm different – I'm odd.

Immediate things, like these grasses,
the flowers in the wood, like these bluebells;
the cats that walk through my country,
like the orphans in church, neatly shod,

wearing black hats and white collars,
that I crouch drawing at Vespers:
these are my objects of worship,
the chattering small-talk of God.

GLOVER'S AIT

For Andrzej Panufnik 1914-1991

Under bowed willows that the heron
conducts, I passed you, where the stream
divides at Glover's Ait. 'Feel dead;
recharging batteries', you said;
smiled and went on, hat raised, the themes
of Thames and Cracow crackling in your head.

Now dead, I see you, son of Poland,
transcribing the angelic jargon
into new orders of the spheres
that resound in your head and ears.
Not dead, we hear you conjure far-gone
wonder and beauty back through floods of tears.

'Recharging batteries', you said.
Recharge your batteries, indeed
as you walk, Andrzej, by the river
you now in heaven's name discover.
Discover all the power you need
to set the antennae of our souls a-quiver.

I see you grip the pen, the baton,
I feel the spark of making leap,
the knowledge of creation start
where birds with rustling crotchets part

the leaves of stillness and of sleep
and set up acclamation in the heart.

Yours are the shining waters that
still pour and trickle through these reeds,
making of rain and mud the great
current of joy and dole; from freight
of Thames and Vistula, choked weeds
washed by hope's flow, work that withstands the spate.

Your father's violins that beat
like humming hearts, as they were taught,
pulse deep in you. A morning that,
like most, seemed undistinguished, flat
as ebb-mud, feels the head of thought,
the gust of the inheritance lift your hat.

BREATH

Mist gathers. Noon grows chill.
Winter is come upon
the Abbey and Soho.
Polluted souls traverse
Smith Street and Ludgate Hill.
Divers we knew are gone
under the wheels and snow,
their breath become a verse.

Breath like a little steam
crosses the frosty air,
spreads itself out in space,
but not to disappear.
Though vapour and mere dream,
it braves the abyss we stare
into at night to place
its bloom beside our fear.

We cherish what we touch
but learn to cherish too
what time or face denies,
beauty that's not for sight.
The word that says so much,
the trembling of what's true,
rises before these eyes
and with such wise delight

breathes on this page I con,
spreads over desk and books,
curls down in thought, re-forms
to be what and with whom
it was in Eden. On
winter's lit bridge it looks
star-mass of brilliants, warms
time, heart's frost, and the tomb.

Sally Purcell

b. 1944; educated at Lady Margaret Hall, Oxford; a student of Medieval French, she has translated and edited a variety of poets, from Charles of Orleans (Carcanet) to D.G. Rosetti's translations of early Italian poets (Anvil), as well as *The Exiles of James Joyce* (Calder). Her own poetry has appeared from various small presses, ranging from Anvil and Taxus to Mammon and Greville. It is a poetry that inhabits a very special domain: the fey, the Arthurian and legendary – the world of Charles Williams and, to a degree, of John Heath-Stubbs – and it sets her apart not only from 'the mainstream' but, in our world of hyper-modern, streetwise poetry, guarantees that it is not so much a poetry of exile as an exiled poetry. John Cotton's essay on her work in the St. James' Press *Contemporary Poets* provides a short, but very illuminating, description of the texture of Sally Purcell's poems when he writes of her 'imaginative insight into the twilight world of superstition, replete with "prodigies and signs of doom" and especially her ability to pinpoint the accompanying physical sensations of such a world... The best way to describe the texture of the verse is that of an intellectual sensuality...' Finally, it is from Sally Purcell that I cull this line (translated via Propertius) which, perhaps, best expresses her view of exile, as well as appositely forming a kind of epigraph for this anthology:

Let others write about you, or else you can stay unknown.

FOR ANDREW

Streams that glitter through new grass
flow from a fountain winter sealed;
now rivers are loosed from the quiet cold
and feed on its bitter snow.

Perceiving a new thaw, poets warily
test bank & dyke, prepare to take the flood
& weave the clear net of channels
that will lead it through the fields.

Without them, waters pour down formless to the sea,
to the blank brightness of a sky,
a dazzle of infinitely moving waves,
to the shore that, opening, leads everywhere,
to exile that is everywhere the same.

ARIADNE

Within this glowing maze Ariadne stands;
a buried city forms her dance's pattern,
her labyrinth is founded on the ruined banks of Troy.

Out of the bittersweet air she leads him,
the king who dances through his fate
in Troy-game, the unchanging order.

His long-told story ripens to an end,
he passes through the final glaring splendour,
and the ancient threads are wound again,
rewoven.

LANCELOT AT ALMESBURY

Here, what was a Queen of Logres
took her to perfection, having lost
everything but one man's worship;
and for two long days, they tell me, her only prayer
was "Let him not see my living face again".

I kept my promise, and never saw my earthly joy again
till now – a young corpse, clothed as a nun.
In a place too cold for tears, I leave her
neither cross nor ring but a branch of white hawthorn.

"AND YOU SHALL FIND ALL TRUE BUT THE WILD ISLAND"

Ariadne regains herself & her solitude –
all she betrayed to the stranger
is vanishing as the black sails dwindle
and he goes forward to found his town.

Where salt-star & rose of sulphur
glitter on the rocks at noon
she has her realm again,
making tiny mazes, Troy-games,
with white pebbles on the sand.

FOR ADVENT

Out from time's tumulus,
        the black bonds laid on Cronos,
Our Lady comes walking
        with a dish full of light,
light that flows through her fingers,
        wavers, ebbs & returns,
between wandering walls of shadow;

Maria, gateway to the great sea,
draws near,
like a sound growing clearer,
bringing together at last
the holly-berry sun
& pearls of mistletoe.

Kathleen Raine

b. 1908 in Ilford, Essex, where she spent her formative years. Through the influence of her mother, who came from the Scottish borders, and through childhood holidays spent in Northumberland, she has assiduously cultivated her affinities with the Celtic Revival. A very English poet she has, nevertheless, woven a complex mythopoeic tapestry of neo-platonic threads around a poetic impulse which derives its nourishment from sources as diverse as Yeats, Shelley, the Vedantic Scriptures of the East, and – above all – William Blake. The style of her poetry, which has been described as 'pure', is that of plain English intoned by the lyra celtica. Apart from her poetry, she is an eminent scholar – especially in Blake studies – but, from her graduation days at Cambridge, she has always been something of an uneasy academic because the dominant philosophical thinking of modern universities, mainly logical positivism, has been inimical to her. Her life has been that of a restless exile, in Chelsea and elsewhere; and like several poets in this volume she has always been, in a sense, both of the 'mainstream', and not of it: famous but unfashionable. In her seventy-third year Kathleen Raine founded *Temenos*, a major journal dedicated to 'The Arts of the Imagination'; and ten years later has developed it into the Temenos Academy, now housed in the Prince of Wales' new Institute for Architecture. Raine is a major poet, but critically neglected; and is perhaps the most formidable female intellect associated with English letters today.

I went out in the naked night
And stood where you had often stood,
And called you where the winter moon
Over Canna harbour rode
Clear of the sheltering wind-bent trees
Above the quivering Pleiades
Where once at anchor rocked your boat.

The mountain isles changeless and still
As memory's insubstantial strand:
May not the living and the dead
Meet where dreaming spirit turns
To the sea-wracked remembered shore,
Revising this welcoming door,
Crushed shells beneath your grounding keel?

The moonlit waters of the bay
Move under the December stars
Between the shores of earth and dream.
In the unending Now of night,
In being's one unbroken theme
Your presence and my present meet:
I hold my transient breath to hear
The crunch of shells beneath your feet.

So many scattered leaves
The Sibyl shakes
From the living tree.
Gather who will her oracles,
Believe who may –
All truths are lies
Save love to love in love replies.

TRIAD

To those who speak to the many deaf ears attend.
To those who speak to one,
In poet's song and voice of bird,
Many listen; but the voice that speaks to none
By all is heard:
Sound of the wind, music of the stars, prophetic word.

THE WILDERNESS

I came too late to the hills: they were swept bare
Winters before I was born of song and story,
Of spell or speech with power of oracle or invocation,

The great ash long dead by a roofless house, its branches rotten,
The voice of crows an inarticulate cry,
And from the wells and springs the holy water ebbed away.

A child I ran in the wind on a withered moor
Crying out after those great presences who were not there,
Long lost in the forgetfulness of the forgotten.

Only the archaic forms themselves could tell
In sacred speech of hoodie on gray stone, or hawk in air,
Of Eden where the lonely rowan bends over the dark pool.

Yet I have glimpsed the bright mountain behind the mountain,
Knowledge under the leaves, tasted the bitter berries red,
Drunk water cold and clear from an inexhaustible hidden fountain.

WITH A WAVE OF HER OLD HAND

With a wave of her old hand
She put her past away,

Ninety years astray
In time's fading land,

With that dismissive gesture
Threw off her pretence,
Rose to her proud stature,
Had done with world's ways,

Had done with words,
Closed her last written book
To ponder deeper themes
In unrecorded dreams.

REMEMBERING FRANCIS BACON

It's not the hells where soul suffers that are eternally
Outside the divine humanity
But the indifferent, the trivial and the vulgar.
Through you we know that our modern Dis
Is a city infinitely terrible,
But from the commonplace
I have learned nothing of the great gulf fixed
Between the nihil and God.

At some party years ago you spoke to me
Of Yeats, and of your sole desire
Once, if only once, to touch the real.
You were speaking from the heart, and I
Who have proclaimed Blake's doctrine of the Divine Body,
Imagination, in which the heavens and hells are redeemed together,
Know that my master would have understood why
You must keep faith with your despair
Who have shown us those dead faces of the damned.
Or am I saying only that you and I
Shared a world, though we seldom met, and therefore
Are bound together
In the unbroken love that runs from friend to friend for ever.

DEVOTEES

(Remembering Maharaj Charan Singh)

Then, when I saw them running to watch him
To the last moment, when his car drove away

I thought, 'Superstitious devotees! I would not!'
But now, his serene turbaned face shining into my room
From a photograph, I think, what a marvel it was
That he lived in this world, and not he
More than many I knew once, whom now I would strain to see
Whom I have treated so casually,
Dear unprized once only
Faces of friends and strangers who have been present to me.

Eric Ratcliffe

b. 1918, saw service in World War 2; a physicist, a bomb-disposal expert, and a Druid, he is best known in the poetry world for his editorship of the long-running small press magazine *Ore,* and as an 'Arthurian enthusiast'. Indeed, Ratcliffe has an especial interest in the 'matter of Britain', and it permeates the majority of his work. Phrases like 'a one off' and 'a true eccentric' come most readily to mind to describe this poet; as well as to account for his marginalisation from poetry's so-called 'mainstream' through all the decades in which he has been writing and editing. To me, Ratcliffe is rarely at his best when writing out of his mytho-historical obsession – then he is at his most indefatigably minor – and, therefore, I prefer to represent him by poems written closer to his actually-lived experience. One of the most satisfactory poems in which his romantic-mystical propensity and eccentric learning come together is 'The Spirit of The Green Light', the very success of which leaves me wondering whether we may yet see some greater mythopoeic work from this poe''s pen comparable, say, to Charles Williams' *Taliessin Through Logres* or Heath-Stubbs' *Artorius*?

THE SPIRIT OF THE GREEN LIGHT

Soft witch, abide and sing,
who lives by the inner and outer oak,
in the waters of life, the Nile,
and all holy rivers:

> with your green light held high, raise
> your maid-arm pointed,
> sing against blood-letting, be of love
> like those who drew water.

Soft witch, abide and sing
of the form printed upon the soul,
the thunder about the lightning,
the flesh on the spirit:

> with your green light held high, shine
> it on the hind and the white hart,
> and on all animals we cut to devour,
> who have faith and no tears in their eyes.

Soft witch, abide and sing
of Moses, Molmutius and Hu Gadarn,
Of Ezra, Howel, and Yesu,
dispensers of white glory:

> and with your green light held high, raise
> your maid-arm pointed,
> sing against violence, and until world's end time
> bless, and bless, and bless the gentle races.

OLD FRAGRANCE

Halting and walking in strange dead seasons
through the weak light of ghost Octobers,
surrendered to the final lute
they sing from melodies unborn.

They have chanted how they remembered
the first sleeping diamonds of dew
on the white flowers left weeping
by the wall in the graveyard dawn.

They have forgotten that instant without breath
in the green midnight glory of cool ferns,
that moment in the lonely bedroom
when a whole heart sighed through curled fingers
and passed between two winds in the corn.

NURSE, TEDDINGTON HOSPITAL

They taught her to cure, not by the cradled arm,
but by the sharpness of heart in face of illness:
she learned the cheerful delicate trade of orders;
to be a tiny clear-centred enquirer
moving from bed to bed on the dull parquet,
bearing the attributes of the absolute
on the shoe of her poised leg.

Yet someone had given her glen talk,
taught her to enclose a sweetness in the husk of words;
to be an artiste before stroke-seared old men
until they felt within their map of bones
the keen warmth of a summer to come,
and knew for a chalice the small glass in their hands.

FLOWER-GIRL, ISLEWORTH HOSPITAL

Like a live signal, a poet should compress her
into a star-cluster in some constellation
for Shaw to admire. For this is another Eliza,
brash, honey-haired, a tawny thruster
straight-backed as a Roman fruit girl,

with a skirt blue as the shouting sky.

Her hand of flowers, struck like a sensual torch
flares in rebellion at the gate.
In a sprat-faced house, rough with kindness,
on a hard bed, she will take her lover
with nine eyes and an open kiss
and a curse for all polite relatives.
She is a tawny thruster, this Eliza.

AGES UNTO AGES

('Our birth is but a sleep and a forgetting...'
– Wordsworth)

White sing the living at evensong
where sounded the tones of the musical dead,
for the night stones bred the old high aura
which bounded the clerestory over their bed.

Heaven was where the old bards spoke,
Hell the reflection of earth-green things;
waxen the faces where blood once flowed
– God's marionettes on artery strings.

Long was the sleep but longer the learning
stretched where unfiltered moonlight wanes
for souls of the bodies of children and children
once under their mothers' counterpanes.

Peter Russell

None of the facts of Russell's life – other than that he was born in Bristol in 1921 – have been simple. An almost-graduate of London University, he became an officer in the army in the war; a publisher; a bookseller; the editor of *Nine*, one of the outstanding literary magazines in the 1950s; a much 'married' man; a bankrupt; Ezra Pound's last significant disciple, and the publisher of Pound's economic pamphlets in English; the drinking pal of 'Talking Bronco' Roy Campbell who, if he did not teach Russell to break horses, certainly taught him to break hearts – satirically; and, above all, a poet and disaster-prone exile. An erudite, prolific poet, he has lived since the early 1960s in Berlin, Venice, British Columbia, Teheran and Tuscany – with short sojourns elsewhere. Russell's untidy corpus of work has tended to attract eulogies or silence – more of the latter than the former. The sole exception to this critical polarisation has been Dick Davis, who wrote: 'It is difficult to get at the substance of Peter Russell's achievement, and the author himself does not make it any easier. Ezra Pound is the first obstacle to be circumnavigated: Russell's public *persona* is so close to Pound's as to seem almost a parody of it; the obscurely allusive verse, the eccentric learning, the tedious reports of skirmishes in the trivial battle between Bohemia and Philistia, the contempt for academia (except when it speaks well of oneself), the mix of languages from which Russell translates…' etc. A negative, if not entirely inaccurate view of Russell, but from a writer unable to grasp the simple fact that Russell at his best (unlike Pound) is a lyric poet in unlyrical times. One driven away from the UK by a critical climate no longer able to respond to the heart, the imagination, the divine intellect, but only to the scientific and socially real, the active fancy, and the unmusicality of a predominantly demotic voice. In an age dominated by poetry competitions, arts council bursaries,moribund publishers, and posh literary festivals run by 'arts administrators', there seems no place for the barbarism of raw genius.

DAUNIA

Generous wick with the oil of the coconut palm
Kindling each evening our nuptial flame,
Witness you were of the love-act a number of times
Nightly, in the city of Sfax in my youthful days,
Till Daunia left me to shiver in an empty bed.
She it was who originally insisted on this
Petting and kissing by lamplight till long after dawn
Made weak the once-upright flame at our bedside.
Possible outcomes or permanency never entered
Our heads that were full of sex-games and gladiators;
The arena by day and the dust of our bed by night
With the trim wick glowing, and the wail of musicians
On the other side of the forum, with flutes and a drum
Loading the evening air with voices and wine,
Kept us too busy for thoughts of a home or of infants.
Now she has left me, now she's run off with another
(Rotten scum of a fellow from Rome with more
Gold in his purse than ever my father had
Before the drachma crashed and the markets went dead), –
With him she's gone off, they leave on the next boat for Rome.
She knocked on my door in the morning to say goodbye
'Don't weep, Quintilius, you will soon find another nice girl
To warm you in bed and wash your hair before sleep.
You'll forget your sweet Daunia long before she
Ceases to long for a former lover in Sfax'.
I couldn't bear to hear more of these words, so quickly
Went out into the backyard with the chickens
And wept, leaving the rest of her message to fall
On the polished brass knocker, my father's pride.
I had often thought I was going to end up a failure;
At the worst I had thought 'This girl will be a good
Wife to me now I'm a failure at everything else
Unbraiding her hair in the evening and lulling our babes
To sleep as the sun goes down on our modest house',
But had never troubled to ask her. Now she has gone,
And the bright streets of Rome will claim her the rest
Of her girlish days. Perhaps I shall die single
Not troubling to cook myself breakfast or
Keep more than a few half-bottles in the house

Of cheap red wine, and a jar of black olives.
Delicacies cost such a lot –
Without her to want an occasional bracelet
I shall die with my palms clean of the dust of gold
And be none the worse off. 'O Mother Venus
What can your poor sons do deserted by girls
They have ever taken for granted? It hurts.
Send either another Greek courtesan
Who is tired of life in the brothels, and is seeking a home
Modest enough for dull me to provide for,
Or end this unnecessary slowness of days.
I'll make her a good husband I promise you;
Just find me a house with a field not too far from the city
With space enough for chickens, a cock, a pig and a cow:
Let it have three or four gnarled and split olive-trees
With ripe berries in early November; let it
Have ample room for the winter-wheat and a terrace
Of large-leaved vines for the summer months.
And don't forget to remind your old father
To make sure there's rain when it's needed. Dear Goddess
I'd soon take root at the edge of the city of Sfax
Provided my new wife doesn't turn out a scold
And further invasions don't interrupt the quick-footed hours
With parties of homeless and hungry looking for food.'
What a fool I was not to ask that girl at the time:
Her soft fingers made sweet our evening food
And she never refused to delight in the joys of Love.
I doubt I shall find another, at least in this age.

OUT OF THE BLIND AND DARK LONG SIEGE OF NIGHT...

Out of the blind and dark long siege of night,
The eyelids shut, the limbs gone dead like stone,
Blood's daytime torrent, molten sun's gold might
Stunned to a sleeping simulacrum, – prone, –
A corpse infused with mouldering aconite,
A stagnant rivulet within the bone
Where the dank marsh exhales a ghastly light,

Cold shadows rise and occupy the Throne.

Anaesthetised, the body lies, a thing
At total standstill, locked the mortal frame,
A slumbering beast deprived of human will, –
But then, illustrious, like an ancient King
Or healing Pharaoh hurling active flame,
The Soul in Triumph rises, calm and still.

SMOKE

'The way the English *professore* smokes! –
A tale to make an alligator weep!
His average is – he's not like other blokes, –
Ninety a day, and sixty in his sleep.'

They say he works in three unstaggered shifts
Without a break, – of reading, writing, *thought*;
Suggesting he's abused his natural gifts
For making money, pretty girls, – and port.

He smokes his way from 6 a.m. till 1
Reading old books and making lengthy notes;
Then cooks up *poems* out of all he's done, –
From then till 8, declining heptaptotes:

And all the while tobacco like a screen
Burnt to blue fibres in the kitchen air,
Drifts like the present past that might have been
A future perfect – world beyond compare.

From 8 to 3 a.m. he rises to his feet
And wraps his thoughts around him like a cloak,
Close as a silent mummy's winding sheet,
Ascends the stairs still in a cloud of smoke;

Removes his shoes and climbs into the bed,
Reads one last page of Wisdom for the night;

Thanks the great Gods for all the Sages said, –
Then stretches out an arm, – and dims the light.

And then this fumigated body sleeps,
And all its fumes like walls it thrusts aside,
Subsides in Soul, a harvest-mouse that creeps
At winter's onset, gently in his hide.

And then Illumination strikes that Mind –
The forms of all things that have been or will
Arise in the arena of the blind
Where all is bright and strange, moving yet still,

Eccentric, shambling like a living corpse
By day, a body spoiled of youth and blood;
By night, King of the risen tribe of Mouldwarps
Flinging apart the prisoning walls of mud, –

Naked among the eternal naked souls
He drinks dread secrets from the Sacred Fount;
Clear in his mind as brightly glowing coals
Beholds such Mysteries mortals daren't recount.

A single image, aeons past mere words,
Unfolds itself before him where he stands,
Beholding all of Wisdom's scattered sherds
Like a great Urn, the womb of Shadowy Lands;

And all the words of all the languages
Join in a single warp to make One Word, –
A giant molecule, that like a swarm of bees
Primaeval Gods in the first Kosmos heard

Descending slowly like a weightless Dove
On the first waters brooding like a World,
Until it burst, disseminating Love,
In boundless seeds like sperm or spindrift hurled.

And all the while that Soul beheld that dive,
That timeless spring from the Divine evoked, –
The body, in its drugged sleep still alive,

Its sixty winters of tobacco – *smoked,*

Till all that Beauty, darkened by the Dream
Fading like stars into the light of Dawn, –
He woke into the smoke of filmy *seem,*
Blind rags and tatters once again reborn.

CALL MAN HAPPY

All day that woman is weaving her wonderful tapestry,
Everything in it in true and beautiful colours.
She is the supreme Enchantress – you cannot doubt the world.
You live according to appearances – how else can you?
What else is there to live in or live for?

And you set out on your journey of touching and tasting,
Of trying to know, of trying to get inside. But you don't.
And the sun's rays stiffen the hairs on the back of your neck,
And it is good. And you walk down the path as though
It were the first day of April though in truth it is the last of December.
But you are happy, whatever that is, but you know that you are –
There's no doubt about that. You are happy. You feel it.
You feel nothing else. You ask for nothing more –
Surely you couldn't have more unless perchance to share
This dream with another. You share the delight of the moment
Out. Half each? Not at all. You each get more
By sharing, than by hogging it all to yourself.
If the clouds come and paste over that source of sunlight
It doesn't matter. Participation in beauty
Persists eternally in memory.

Tom Scott

b. Glasgow 1918. The last of the modern *makars* of the Scottish Literary Renaissance inaugurated by Hugh MacDiarmid. On his own admission a sort of 'natural convert' to writing in Scots; but he remains a skilful versifier in English. More at home in the long poem than the short, Scott is nevertheless sufficiently attuned to the lyra celtica to produce fine lyric poems from time to time. In many ways a Scottish Villon (his first publication being some remarkable translations of that French master), Tom Scott has – on account of the strength of his views, and willingness to commit them to print – been for many years outside the established pale, an exile in his own land. Of the many Scots in our century who have written in 'Lallans', it is my view that only MacDiarmid, Sidney Goodsir-Smith, Robert Garioch, and Tom Scott have been able to develop distinct voices in it: in Tom Scott's case nowhere more so than in his marvellous poetical character-study Brand. According to the Scots' critic George Bruce: '*Brand The Builder* stands at the heart of Tom Scott's achievement. The language is a rich Scots vernacular, dignified by the formality of a verse that is sufficiently free to allow the direct speech of Brand to arise naturally out of it'. As the publisher of that work in England, I can but agree, and also draw attention to the fact that it is a tribute to the poet that – unlike many other writers in Scots – Scott has managed to gain some readership south of the Border. A fact further testified to by the publication of an earlier important volume *The Ship and Ither Poems* by O.U.P. in 1963; the publication of the aforementioned Villon translations also in England; the special issue of *Agenda* magazine devoted to his work in 1993; and a superbly-edited *Collected Shorter Poems Of Tom Scott* which that magazine, in conjunction with *Chapman,* brought out in the same year. Though his 'ear' has always been good, his principal weakness has been a tendency to descend into rant – always the risk of the didactic poet. This has contributed greatly to his neglect.

BRAND THE BUILDER

On winter days, aboot the gloamin hour,
When the nock on the college touer
Is chappan lowsin-time,
And ilka mason packs his mell and tools awa
Under his banker, and, bien forenenst the waa
The labourer haps the lave o the lime
Wi soppan sacks, to keep it frae a frost, or faa
O suddent snaw
Duran the nicht;
When scrawnie craws flap in the shell-green licht
Towards yon bane-bare rickle o trees
That heeze
Up on the knowe abuin the toun,
And the red goun
Is happan mony a student frae the snell nor-easter,
Malcolm Brand, the maister,
Seean the last hand throu the yett
Afore he bars and padlocks it,
Taks yae look aroond his stourie yaird
Whaur chunks o stane are liggan
Like the ruins o some auld-farrant biggin;
Picks a skelf oot o his baerd,
Scliffs his tacketty buits, and syne
Clunters hamelins doun the wyn'.

Doun by the sea
Murns the white swaw owre the wrack ayebydanlie.

The main street echoes back his fuitfaas
Frae its waas
Whaur owre the kerb and causeys, yellow licht
Presses back the mirk nicht
As shop fronts flude the pavin-stanes in places
Like the peintit faces whures pit on, or actresses,
To please their different customers.

Aye the nordren nicht, cauld as rumour
Taks command,
Chills the toun wi his militarie humour,

And plots his map o starns wi felloun hand.

Alang the shore
The greenan white sea-stallions champ and snore.

Stoopan throu the anvil pend
Gaes Brand,
And owre the coort wi the twa-three partan-creels,
The birss air fu
o the smell o the sea, and fish, and meltit glue;
Draws up at his door, and syne,
Hawkan his craig afore he gangs in ben,
Gies a bit scart at the grater wi his heels.

The kail-pat on the hob is hotteran fu
Wi the usual hash o Irish stew,
And by the grate, a red-haired bewtie frettit thin,
His wife is kaaain a spurtle roond.
He swaps his buits for his baffies but a soond.

The twa-three bairns ken to mak nae din
When faither's in,
And sit on creepies roond aboot.
Brand gies a muckle yawn
And howks his paper oot.

Tither side the fire
The kettle hums and mews like a telephone wire.

> "Lord, for what we are about to receive
> Help us to be truly thankful – Aimen:
> Woman ye've pit ingans in't again!"
>
> "Gae wa, ye coorse auld hypocrite,
> Thank the Lord for your meat syne grue at it!"

Wi chowks drawn ticht in a speakless sconner
He glowers on her,
Syne on the quate and strecht-faced bairns:
Faulds his paper doun aside his eatin-airns
And, til the loud tick-tockin o the nock

Sups, and reads wi nae other word nor look.

The warld ootside
Like a lug-held seashell, sings wi the rinnan tide.

The supper owre, Brand redds up for the nicht.
Aiblins there's a schedule for to price
Or somethin nice
On at the picters – secont hoose –
Or some poleetical meetin wants his licht,
Or aiblins, wi him t-total aa his life
And no able to seek a pub for relief frae the wife,
Daunders oot the West Sands "on the loose".
Whitever tis,
The waater shorps frae his elbuck as he synds his phiz.

And this is aa the life he kens there is?

THE DEATH O BRAND

Deid this day ligs the builder Brand
But villa, hall, and steeple stand;
His mell and chisel are useless lain,
Yet nae tears coorse frae the hert o stane.

His bevel, troon, and plumbline tae
Lig in the kist as uselessly
As in the grave the lifeless bane:
Yet nae tears coorse frae the hert o stane.

His yerd is as desertit nou
As some auld citie in Peru:
A king is bye wi't, and his reign,
Yet nae tears coorse frae the hert o stane.

The heidtsanes in this plot o grund
Nae mair nou will ken his hand
Carve the dictates o his brain:
But nae tears coorse frae the hert o stane.

A hert o stane ye'd need to hae
To feel nae stound for Brand the-day.
The builder's enterit on his ain,
But nae tears coorse frae the hert o stane.

But I'm nae stane, and here I stand
Wi stangan hert for Malcolm Brand
Whase like I'll never see again
Till tears coorse frae the hert o stane.

LOVE IN ELD

Affection more than passion is my love now,
The gentler love that mellowing years can bring.
    The lust of youth now rarely bothers
    Me, and the touch of my hand is tender.

Caressing, not possessing, is my embrace.
My heart could not endure the tormented love
    That once it knew, but now no longer
    Suffers, the rage of the blood is over.

But love is in me still, though a milder kind,
As swallows touch in air, or as mating swifts,
    And then fly on, or as wayfarers
    Meet and converse, before passing onward.

And I've a house whose door I keep open for
Those rarer beings who are my soul's true kin,
    With food and drink, and rest for weary
    Hearts, and a glow in the fire if wanted.

I promise nothing but that you'll always find
Such welcome here, if you should choose to come,
    Your coming free, and free your going
    Hence, like the wind on the moorland blowing.

LET GO WHO WILL

In this time I would ask three things
    As the solitudes round me close:
Spare but the sensitive nerve that sings,
    The stormcock and the rose.

For none I can lose are really lost,
    Traitor no friend can be:
Bury the dead and forget the cost,
    Love only who stand with me.

Let all those go that want to go,
    Let only the leal remain:
The half and half would melt like snow
    Or as ice dissolves in the rain.

Donald Ward

b. 1909 in Surrey; educated at St. George's School, Ramsgate, spent his whole working life as a postman: apt if one considers how much poets depend on the postal service! Ward learned his craft, like so many, as a member of 'The Group' run by Edward Lucie Smith, and its successor 'Poetry Workshop'. When Allison & Busby published his first volume *The Dead Snake* in 1971 it won an Arts Council Award, the poet was profiled in a national newspaper, and it looked as if one 'late developer', or, at least, one late to publishing, had become 'established'. After the demise of Allison & Busby, Anvil Press produced *Border Country*, and there were pamphlets from Mandeville and Mammon, yet – perhaps through the 'exile of age' (though this usually increases rather than decreases a poet's reputation) – Ward's star sank quietly back into the world of little magazines. (Though it has recently revived somewhat with a new volume from Hippopotamus Press.) It may be that Ward – very much a writer in the nature tradition of Wordsworth and Edward Thomas – 'lost out' in an era increasingly given over to the Martian cleverness of Craig Raine and the barbarous realism of Peter Reading. Whatever the reason for his neglect, there is much that is truly fine in his limited output, and its only identifiable weaknesses are a tendency here and there towards minimalism which, unlike the same tendency in Peter Dale's work, has proved more stultifying than liberating; and a habit of producing too many poems that operate solely on the descriptive level.

THE WARD

Acholoona, Chilalika,
who would not be nursed by these,
Or Guana
chic and slender
laughing through her walls of pearls,

or by Zasu, self-effacing,
grey marigolds – and
dying eyes –
or by Slaithwaite, cool Athena,
when the sea has lost
its tides,

or by Runford
from Snowdonia, and all
the gnashing of the winds –
or the green-lit ghost that wanders
with her dubious
final dream,

or the classic, morning sister
with her formal, neat
replies – or the
matron made of marble
trailing sister
with her 'slide',

or the last remote Messiah
with his titularistic ploy,
with his wisdom and
his half-truth,
half-confession,
half a lie.

DARENTH VALLEY

The thin wires harp on the breeze,
Bird song is faint and out of sight;
Birds hide in trees or are screened by the hedge,
In the long grass birds are tongues.

And beyond the hedge the wide fields
Create those sleeping distances
Which rise into the wooded hills
Where a few rooks are circling trees.

And from this gate, browsing corn,
I see the voiceless swallows fly
And the stiff sparrows frequently
Shoot by in pairs, home everywhere.

And in full trees the ring doves fill
The air with softness. As they fall
Shattering the silence with their flight
They leave the silence in their wake.

NORTH DOWNS

The heat in a thin mist holds the hills;
Beyond the next tree the barley moves
Softly as a snail... occasionally
Sibilant, sibilant – through the antennaed ears.

The great trees pile their foliage now;
Mid-dark, mid-summer, turning round.
Mindless, mindless, in the still heat
Each sound is its own possession now.

Even the plane with its barbarous whine
And sublime nonchalance is a sigh
Drowned in the blue, ethereal blue,
Wearing the sun upon its hull.

Now speed is almost still, and still
I watch the liner out of sight –
Concrete, and yet mystical
Till silence almost drops like night.

More silent still, more velvet-kind,
I trace the fields that spread their view,
The tender valley rolls with shade –
The massive delicacy of the hills.

THE DAMSELFLY

Gloom filters to wood-light,
a closeness, not sultry, almost cool –
waist-deep of growth
through widening caverns

till softly, suddenly, the pool
– a shimmer of jewels.
Blue, almost still,
suspended – yet moving,

silent as a dream
the damselfly
hangs blueness
on water.

Silent as a dream
or a gleam of the sun
through the half-light
gloom of the wood

bulrushes stand, useful,
solid as trees;
velvet, real –
but the damselfly

is too thin to be real, too blue –

electric – yet tranquil,
tranquil, yet never
quite still –

it floats rather than moves,
glides, picked out by the sun, it has
nothing to offer the world
but itself.

Francis Warner

b. Yorkshire 1937; educated at Christ's Hospital; nine years at Cambridge University before taking up an academic post at St. Peter's College, Oxford. A deeply tradition-conscious poet-playwright, somewhat academically reclusive, and largely content in the current of his admiration for poets like Shakespeare, Blunden, Yeats. Genuinely indifferent to 'the taste of the time', with an occasional tendency to pastiche, even in his most passionate lucubrations. A verse-playwright in the style of Yeats, Warner sought, in his earlier stage work, to import a major Beckettesque element which sat uneasily with his splendid Georgianism, consequently his later plays – for all their beautiful versifying – tend to the dramatically static. Nevertheless, scattered throughout his plays, especially his 'history plays', there is fine poetry.

The stanzas introducing his *Collected Poems, 1960-1984* well express the shaping spirit of this academic-oriented poet, and I quote from these:

> I give a tongue to my accustomed streets,
> The buildings two slow rivers wind among;
> Cambridge's sun-touched world of youth and song
> That mellow Oxford's majesty completes.
>
> ...
>
> For these two holy cities set apart
> In meditation undeterred by time
> Have been the shaping parents of my art,
> Shown me their truth, and truth her paradigm:

But 'places' apart, and outside of his plays – where demands of narrative and dialogue from time to time call forth a more objective, less personal, poetry – Warner's principal themes are romantic-erotic experiences and a pastoral view of nature. Like A.L. Rowse – but for somewhat different reasons – Francis Warner must be classed as self-exiled.

SONNET FOR KOINONIA

I went to Binsey but you were not there,
Although the sun still warmed unshadowed lawns.
I watched the white doves strut around the chair
And wasps spill beer and chutney in their swarms.
Restless I walked where river weeds had grown,
Preoccupied with thoughts of you away
In a far country, unattached, alone –
My music with no instrument to play.
I left September bundle up in bales
And climbed the library where every dusk
I'd find you stooped among your travellers' tales
High up in Bodley, like an owl in musk.
    Binsey or Bodley, by our books or stream,
    Delight's pale shadow is my cherished gleam.

A towel; suitcase; this a hotel room.
Each object, élite, curiously numb:
Clean, empty place of unreality,
All singly neat. Mad traffic hurtling on,
Metal, below. The bed's bare winding-sheets.
Alone for time to come: then why sit down
To throw an understatement on a page –
How can I further explore heartbreak's pit
And come back sane? No: let the new scab form;
Stay numb. Cross-lock the door. Force the hand still;
Unless articulation stir, to fill
The icy moment at the heart of pain.
    Is there a reason behind human care?
    What is the acreage of its despair.

Should we preserve intensity alone?
The string vibrating at the 'cello's bridge?
Or stretch to nerve the fingerboard's full range

In orchestrating waste's cacophonics?
Is poignancy of beauty's transience
As time runs over an apple in the stream –
The hesitancy of a summer's dusk
When night-stock stuns with scent – ours to forgo?
Must we desert court-ladies on the grass,
Their sunlit-dappled breasts and lovers' lutes?
The skill of craftsman-wrought, firm, rounded themes;
The guests of Mozart, Purcell, and Watteau?
    Bear with me if I leave such scenes behind:
    The dark offstage preoccupies my mind.

THE BALLAD OF BRENDAN BEHAN

Come gather round me, sweethearts,
    And lovers, lift your heads;
Come, old men from the fireside,
    And children from your beds;
Come, neighbours, friends, and travellers,
    And hear me sing a stave
Of a laughing boy from Dublin
    Now lying in his grave.

For Brendan loved his city,
    The place where he was born,
He'd toast her health in Mooney's
    From twilight round till morn;
From morn again to twilight
    He'd laugh and sing and say
'Mock all the world, my darlin's,
    But back the I.R.A.'

They put him into prison
    When he was sweet fifteen,
And innocent of whiskey,
    And only knew potheen:
In Liverpool they locked him
    For smuggling contraband,

For forging of a passport,
    And fighting for his land.

Eight long years being over,
    The Borstal boy was free;
He kissed the screws and sold his shoes
    To sail the homeward sea.
He quenched his English prison thirst
    With English prison pay,
And wrote a laughing prison book,
    And then a hanging play.

Joan Littlewood in London,
    She sent a telegram:
'Come join us in our theatre,
    Come back, me darlin' man!'
Soon Brendan's name is blazoned
    In flashing neon lights.
The laughing boy buys drinks for all
    Throughout the winter nights.

He scribbled as he gargled
    Another singing play,
About a cockney soldier
    Shot by the I.R.A.
His fame crossed the Atlantic,
    His laughter shook New York:
But still he loved his Dublin,
    His Galway, and his Cork.

A Gaelic baby daughter
    Grinned up a new-born smile:
'Be Jasus! I'll forsake the malt
    And take up milk awhile.'
He snatched his pen, and wrote again
    Two books about his friends,
Then quaffed a can at The Shaky Man
    To join and make amends.

Oh all you wives and lovers,
    Take heed unto my tale;

Follow the fate of the laughing boy
    Locked in an English gaol;
The boy with laughter in his eyes,
    And liquor in his veins:
And love like him, forgive like him,
    Till Death knocks out your brains.

THE UNIVERSE SPINS ON A SHAFT OF LIGHT

The universe spins on a shaft of light
    Whose name is love.
Flowers of the meadows folded up all night
    Spread for high strength above
Them, warming out their secrets till
Displayed for all to see each world's a daffodil.

Full-blown with morning, laughing to the sky
    With puckered lips
They kiss sun's mastery to catch his eye.
    No night-jar trips
Among the undergrowth between the stars,
For violets and primrose chain the bars.

I took a prism, dazzled as a king,
    And held it up.
Light shattered into all the flowers of spring.
    Kingcup
And stalked marsh-marigold, its spendthrift son,
Transfigured all around till night and day were one.

What vision have I seen? Flowers wheel like suns
    In daisy-chains of dance
Round daffodils, whose green-gold laughter stuns
    To ignorance
My day-dull thoughts. Then suddenly the clue
To all was clear. That source of light is you.

Julie Whitby

Following the policy-lead given by T.S. Eliot – who 'liked to see a poet appearing in the little magazines before considering a collection' – Faber, for many years after Eliot's death, seemed to restrict that rule of thumb, rather snobbishly, to journals like *The Times Literary Supplement, Encounter, The New Statesman, The Spectator,* or *The Poetry Review*. Well, Julie Whitby's work has, for over two decades, found a home in many of these 'right places'. *Agenda* – the most distinguished, if not the most influential, of 'little magazines' since *The Review* – has consistently supported her work. Yet, until last year, she never had a collection of poems. At a guess this was because her often tenderly romantic poetry – romantic even unto decadence – had not been able to buck the trend of awful, street-wise realism that predominates today in book publishing; whereas a magazine can, of course, afford the occasional poem or two which are outside 'the accepted contemporary canon' or manufactured 'taste of the time'. Yet neither the subsidized specialist presses, nor the London publishers – it must be presumed – were willing to go against the grain. For to do so would, doubtless, have meant many things, including a greater oppenness to feeling (romantic-spiritual-subjective) than editors – who appear to be either academically-trained ironists bred in the Movement tradition, or coarse-grained logo louts – can bear. Yet is it not now time to recall that most literate of artists Van Gogh's words on the matter of the supposed conflict between romanticism and realism? He wrote 'Romance and romanticisim are of our time. Luckily realism and naturalism are not free from it. Zola creates, but does not hold a *mirror* to things, he creates *wonderfully*: Poeticises.' Julie Whitby well understands this.

OUTDOOR CAFÉ, PEN AND PROSE IN HAND

Never green so green on trees that deride
my rag-bag hide. Staid tables squeak
as placidly an attendant wipes them clean.
Oh painfully inside I cry:
can't I do the same for me, whimpering why?

It's that long-standing, friendly enemy,
the homely goddess emotion:
observe her coffee stain
both outside and in.

And still the words that need to be said
can't come, don't speak,
yet constantly mutter, splutter away
tightly contained within my head,
and instead: 'Sorry, after you… don't worry',
peeling the pants off, but nothing else.

Yes, an assertive lawnmower persecutes
a crowd of forgotten daffodils
their brown heads shrivelled and bowed,
destroys their uneven, dusty peace with mine:
brazenly recalling manslaughter of summers' past
when youth, but not love, was allowed.

Never green so green on trees that deride
my rag-bag pride and love, unlooked for, golden.
Yet the words needing to be said
shriek their rebuke, with rage purple and sage,
their curses tender as lead –
inside, oh inside my head!

And the daffodils, once so bright and self-assured,
oh teasing…
They're no longer listening, even.
Didn't you notice
how quiet they are, now they're dead?

ALL THE LONG DAY

(for my mother)

I wake to the desolation
of knowing I'll not see you again.
How unfeelingly then I treated you,
how fiercely tender I've since become.

All the long day
your love flowed without hesitation –
but my stupid heart lay numb.

Now I wake to a stormy desolation:
through clouds of memory, of remorse,
sense the blue of dawn cannot return,
has tunelessly changed to dun.

NO MORE THE OLD SADNESS

Together we welcome the day –
no more the old sadness –
two ships calm in the bay,
yet bright with their journeying.

Together we embrace our day:
bodies close and loving,
green light of trees mingles with sun,

we drink our honied tea at ease, in freedom,
for time has only just begun.
Who could ask for more?
Two ghosts flit across the floor.

AFTER "THE ROAD IN LOUVECIENNES"

by Camille Pissarro

Do you remember that road in Louveciennes?
The trees taut with their secrets,
and the road tight with snow?

We were close but not touching, as though
what we had was enough, we already knew
all that we needed to know.

How far from reality the road in Louveciennes!
You, a cypress in your dark green dress,
and I, in what my grandfather might have worn,
quaintly mysterious.

How sure the future seemed on our road in Louveciennes:
a sweet cold apple for us to eat.
Those trees, too, would tell us their secrets,

the snow bless us with blossom –
we were close but not touching,
ignorant of love's need, of the drab tread of years.

Do you remember, oh my love, the road in Louveciennes?
Before it grows dark we must find it somehow,
and clasp each other close, since
only we can weep real, unpainted tears.

LINCOLN'S INN FIELDS: HOME TO THE HOMELESS

A purple blanket under filigree leaves,
soft April petals pink the grass that's floor –
not quite the idyll that it was before:
a homeless pair about a brazier shift their feet.

It's noisier now that dusk is here.
They're out from tents which strew sheer grass.

Or from wherever, wherever else
bare days are shivered through.

A man checks half-a-dozen blankets,
prepares methodically for night,
as pigeons (pastoral) coo; and ghostly, white,
tulips quaintly bless an eerie scene

(on the night that Messiian and Francis Bacon died).
More wood is piled upon the fire
'till its mesmeric banner reaches higher
than a child of ten could leap

as it crackles in its sexual trance.
At a closer look those tulips are skeletal,
picked by birds. And now a van like an ambulance
arrives. They gather unmistakably: food?

But it's clothes they're handling, greedily.
I've had enough, it's getting chilly.
Not quite the idyll that it was before,
I'll head for home. And for the first time –
look – a rat is leading the way.

Acknowledgements

For permission to print or reprint the poems in this anthology, and acknowledgement of place of first publication where appropriate, thanks are due to the following:

Anna Adams: To the author; and Littlewood Press for 'Black-House Woman' from *An Island Chapter* , and Peterloo Poets for 'A Burial At Horton' from *Trees In Sheep Country*.

Sebastian Barker: To the author; and Free Man's Press Editions Ltd. for 'Tilty Mill' from *Boom*, Martin Brian & O'Keefe Ltd. for 'Hungover In Henley' from *A Fire In The Rain*, and Enitharmon Press for 'Bluebells' from *Guarding The Border*.

Fred Beake: To the author; and University of Salzburg Press for 'It Was On A Day Of White Frost', 'Signs' and 'I Came To This Cafe' from *The Whiteness Of Her Becoming*.

Anne Beresford: To the author; and Agenda Editions for 'Distance' and 'December' from *The Curving Shore*, and Poetry Now for 'Rain' from *An Anthology Of East Anglian Poetry*.

Heather Buck: To the author; and Anvil Press for 'Moving House' from *At The Window*, and *Acumen* for 'Epiphany'.

Douglas Clark: To the author; and The Benjamin Press for 'Young Brock' from *Dysholm*, for 'Seventeen' and 'Twenty, Thirty, Forty' from *Coatham*, for 'from Love Sonnets' from *Troubadour*.

Jack Clemo: To the author and the estate of Jack Clemo; and Methuen for 'The Plundered Fuchsias' from *The Map Of Clay*, *Cornish Banner* for 'Moor Hunt', and *Acumen* for 'T.E, Lawrence'.

Michael Croshaw: To the author and University of Salzburg Press for poems from *A Harmony Of Lights* and to *Orbis* for 'The Madonnas', *The Magpie's Nest* for 'Spring At Cannon Hill', and to *Thursdays* for 'Friday Night'.

Peter Dale: To the author; and Hippopotamus Press for 'Minutiae', 'Gifts' and 'Will' from *Earthlight*, and Agenda Editions for 'Lullaby' from *Mortal Fire*.

Peter Dent: To the author; and *Iron*, *Tribune*, *New Signature* and Blackthorn Press's *Undergrowth* for 'Windows', 'Recognition' and 'College Withdrawal', and *Delta* and Blackthorn Press's *Contour And Grain* for 'Arc, 1945', and *Outposts* for 'First Thing'.

Feyyaz Fergar: To the Estate of Feyyaz Fergar, and The Rockingham Press for 'Words Are Ancestors', 'Testament', and 'Trust' from *A Talent For Shrouds*, and for 'The Street' and 'Vanity' from *The Bright Is Dark Enough*.

Geoffrey Godbert: To the author; and The Diamond Press for 'Nothing', 'Becoming', 'Lascivious Aubrey Beardsley, Only 25' and 'At This Last Time Of Day' from *Journey To The Edge Of Light*, and Only Poetry Publications for 'In Pictures' from *The Lover Will Dance Incredibly*, and The Diamond Press for 'I Want To Be Young Again' and 'We Are Upstairs Tonight' from *I Was Not, Was Not Mad Today*.

Robert Greacen: To the author; and The Dedalus Press for the poems from *A Bright Mask*.

David H.W. Grubb: To the author; and Headland Publications for 'Departures' from *Somewhere There Are Trains*, *Acumen* for 'The Church In Winter', *Ambit* for 'Hedgehog', *Samphire* for 'The Day Of The Dancing Bear', and *Rialto* and University of Salzburg Press for 'Turtle Mythologies'.

Harry Guest: To the author; and *Acumen* and Anvil Press's volume *Coming To Terms* for 'Florida Sunset', 'A Daughter's First Term At University', and 'Then And Now'; and *Slow Dancer* for 'Wales Re-Visited'.

John Gurney: To the author; and Acumen Publications for 'Miss Rossetti At Cheyne Walk' from *An Average Revenge*.

John Heath-Stubbs: To the author; and Carcanet New Press for 'Ibycus', 'A Charm Against Toothache', 'Shepherd's Bush Eclogue', 'To Edmund Blunden', and 'Moving To Winter' from *Collected Poems*.

A.C. Jacobs: To the author and the estate of A.C. Jacobs; and Hearing Eye for 'Out' and 'Please Note' from *A Bit Of Dialect* and Tim Gee Editions for 'Poem For My Grandfather', 'Jerusalem' and 'Sound' from *The Proper Blessing*.

James Kirkup: To the author; and Oxford University Press for 'Transatlantic Flight' from *A Spring Journey & Other Poems*, and for 'Wreath Makers: Leeds Market' and 'Swan Legends' from *A Correct Compassion*; and Rockingham Press for 'The Sand Artist' and 'Variations On A Theme By Robert Desnos' from *Throwback*.

Lotte Kramer: To the author; and Hippopotamus Press for 'On Reading Some News Before A Train Journey', 'Women In Dress Shops' and 'The Last Of Winter' from *A Lifelong House*, Annakin for 'Aspects Of Home' from *Ice-Break*, *Acumen*, *The Jewish Quarterly* and Rockingham Press for 'Cocoon', and *Outposts* and *The Jewish Chronicle* for 'Bilingual'.

Dinah Livingstone: To the author; and Rivelin Grapheme Press for 'To My Camden Poetry Group' from *Saving Grace*, Katabasis for 'Woman In Dressing Gown' from *Keeping Heart*, and for 'Rowan Trees' and 'St. Pancras Lock' from *Second Sight*.

Edward Lowbury: To the author; and University of Salzburg Press and Hippopotamus Press for 'The Night Watchman', 'Spring-Cleaning At Seventy', 'In The Train', 'An Old Photograph', and to *Agenda* for 'Spectre Of A Rose'.

Alexis Lykiard: To the author; and to Stride Publications for 'The Art Of Captaincy', 'Advice To A New Writer', 'A Future For Alexander' from *Safe Levels*, and Westwords Publications for 'Second Thoughts' from *Beautiful Is Enough*, and Spacex Literature for 'Distractions' from *Food For The Dragon*.

Richard O'Connell: To the author; and *The Paris Review* for 'Annunciation', *The New Yorker* for 'Stopover In Belém', and *Acumen* for 'North'; and the University of Salzburg Press in whose volume *Retro Worlds* all the poems appeared.

Brian Louis Pearce: To the author; and Woodruff Press for 'Thames Listener' and 'Runaways' from *The Vision Of Piers Librarian*, Tallis Press for 'To Vèra Oumançoff' from *Gwen John Talking*, and Stride Publications for 'Breath' from *Emotional Geology*.

Sally Purcell: To the author; and Anvil Press for 'For Andrew' and 'Ariadne' from *Dark Of Day*, Taxus Press for 'Lancelot At Almesbury' from *Lake And Labyrinth*, and *Verso* (Université de Lyon) for 'And You Shall Find All True But The Wild Island' and 'For Advent'.

Kathleen Raine: To the author; and George Allen & Unwin for 'I Went Out Into The Naked Night...', 'So Many Scattered Leaves...', 'Triad', 'The Wilderness', 'With A Wave Of Her Old Hand', from *Collected Poems 1935-1980*, and *Temenos* for 'Remembering Francis Bacon' and 'Devotees'.

Eric Ratcliffe: To the author; and Ore Publications for 'Nurse, Teddington Hospital' and 'Flower Girl, Isleworth Hospital' from *Leo Poems*, The Mitre Press for 'The Spirit Of The Green Light' and 'Old Fragrance', and *Acumen* for 'Ages Unto Ages'.

Peter Russell: To the author; and Anvil Press for 'Daunia' from *The Elegies Of Quintilius* and for 'Smoke' from *All For The Wolves*, and to *Littack* for 'Out Of The Blind And Dark Long Siege Of Night' and 'Smoke'.

Tom Scott: To the author; and The Ember Press for 'Brand The Builder' and 'The Death o Brand' from *Brand The Builder*, *Littack* for 'Let Go Who Will', and *Agenda* for 'Love In Eld'.

Donald Ward: To the author; and Anvil Press for 'Darenth Valley' from *Border Country*,

Hippopotamus Press for 'North Downs' and 'The Damselfly' from *Lark Over Stone Walls*, and to *Littack* for 'The Ward'.

Francis Warner: To the author; and Colin Smythe Ltd., for all the poems, which are taken from *Collected Poems 1960-1984*, and Anglia TV for 'The Ballad Of Brendan Behan' which was first transmitted on 20th March 1964.

Julie Whitby: To the author; and *Acumen* for 'Outdoor Cafe, Pen And Prose In Hand' and 'All The Long Day', and *Agenda*, *The Independent* and Acumen Publications for 'No More The Old Sadness' and 'After "The Road In Louveciennes"'.

The Editor

William Oxley was born in Manchester in 1939. He has worked as an accountant, gardener and actor, and edited or co-edited a number of books and periodicals in Britain and abroad. Since 1976, when he moved to Devon, he has devoted the greater part of his life to writing – especially poetry. His recent books of poetry include *In The Drift Of Words* (Rockingham Press); *Cardboard Troy* (Stride); and his *Collected Longer Poems* (University of Salzburg Press). Of *Completing The Picture* he comments: 'Assembling this volume has given me greater pleasure than any of my other works'.